PRIME TIME

PRIME TIME

Maximizing the Therapeutic Experience
A Primer for Psychiatric Clinicians

Frederick G. Guggenheim

Routledge
Taylor & Francis Group
New York   London

Routledge
Taylor & Francis Group
270 Madison Avenue
New York, NY 10016

Routledge
Taylor & Francis Group
2 Park Square
Milton Park, Abingdon
Oxon OX14 4RN

© 2009 by Taylor & Francis Group, LLC
Routledge is an imprint of Taylor & Francis Group, an Informa business

Printed in the United States of America on acid-free paper
10 9 8 7 6 5 4 3 2 1

International Standard Book Number-13: 978-0-415-80109-6 (Softcover) 978-0-415-80203-1 (Hardcover)

Library of Congress Cataloging-in-Publication Data

Guggenheim, Frederick G.
    Prime time : maximizing the therapeutic experience : a primer for psychiatric clinicians / by Frederick G. Guggenheim.
        p. ; cm.
    Includes bibliographical references and index.
    ISBN 978-0-415-80203-1 (hardback : alk. paper) -- ISBN 978-0-415-80109-6 (pbk. : alk. paper)
        1. Psychotherapists--Time management. 2. Psychotherapy--Practice. I. Title. II. Title: Maximizing the therapeutic experience.
        [DNLM: 1. Psychotherapy, Brief--methods. 2. Mental Disorders--therapy. 3. Professional-Patient Relations. 4. Time Management--methods. WM 420.5.P5 G942p 2009]

    RC465.5.G84 2009
    616.89'140068--dc22
                                                    2008054210

Visit the Taylor & Francis Web site at
http://www.taylorandfrancis.com

and the Routledge Web site at
http://www.routledge.com

Contents

Introduction

This is a primer. It is intended to help the mental health clinician: practicing psychiatrist and resident, psychologist, psychiatric social worker, psychiatric nurse clinician. The focus is to assist the time-pressured clinician to do *more* (quality work) with *less* (time). Many of us were not trained in how to hurry or how to be efficient, but we were berated if we were too slow. When money counts in training programs, in private practices, all too often the 50-minute hour gets shrunk to the 20-minute hour for follow-up appointments.

In Part 1, there are a variety of shortcuts and experience-tested ways to maximize those 20-minute (or so) sessions so that you and your patient can enjoy the encounter, based on your clinical caring, your art, and your skill, for example: how to use small talk at the beginning to enhance rapport; how to very quickly measure symptoms in assessing depression, anxiety, and lethality; how to set a contract early on that takes little time but explains behaviors that might undercut therapeutic work; how to jump start psychoeducation; shortcuts, including how to end on time; how to deal with terminations. The focus of this primer is to help the clinician as he or she is struggling to keep on schedule by being more time-efficient yet also feeling the pleasure that comes from giving first-rate care in a partnership with patients.

In Part 2, the primer gives snippets of relevant information on a variety of troubling issues that patients bring to therapy: anger, violence, puzzling somatic symptoms, very recent physical trauma, suicidal ideation. There are also technical problems in a non-specialized mental health practice that can perplex the clinician: how to deal with the adolescent, the mentally retarded patient, the patient being stalked. There is also some very up-to-date material on how to deal with the depressed patient, whether unipolar or bipolar. Many research papers on this topic have been written, but still the prescriber often feels that the decision-making process is a random walk.

Textbooks, journals, and the Internet allow for ready focus on *Diagnostic and Statistical Manual of Mental Disorders* (DSM-IV) disorders. But ready information on certain dilemmas that can erupt in clinical practice may be hard to come by, since such information does not lend itself to rapid searching, for example: the questionably psychotic patient, the possibly pregnant patient, the patient with borderline traits, the depressed patient that just doesn't get better, the anxious patient that keeps on resisting any new solutions. When such conditions suddenly emerge, Part 2 of this primer provides a wise supervisor's guidance as you orient your thinking on how best to navigate this new situation. The last three chapters of this primer focus on what to do when the truly terrible happens to you.

This work has come from decades of experience, working with and learning from residents, medical students, nurses, social workers, psychologists, chaplains, and my own patients at academic medical centers, in a community mental health center, and now at a private psychiatric hospital with a residency training program.

Preface

The 20-Minute Hour Is New. Where Did It Come From?

Diligent clinicians never seem to have enough hours in the day, or minutes in the session with their patients. "So much to do and so little time." This current phase of practice is overburdened by requirements for augmented documentation that seemingly detracts from patient care. Additionally, many clinicians are faced with increasing productivity requirements.

The Preface provides a historical review of the changes in practice over the past four decades. Psychotherapy, at times coupled with medication management, gradually has changed from being a relatively leisurely paced but intense pursuit to one that is admittedly much more time-pressured. What was the 50-minute hour has often morphed into the 20-minute hour, or even less, the 15-minute med check.

For psychotherapists and psychiatrists, during the first six decades of the 20th century, there were two certainties. Outpatient sessions lasted 50 minutes and fees were clinician-set, with no support from health insurance. As will be shown, these certainties have mostly evaporated.

THE 50-MINUTE HOUR

Apparently it was Freud who advised his fellow analysts to chill out or cool off for a few minutes between therapeutic hours. Thus the tradition developed that almost all sessions lasted 50 minutes.

Even psychoanalyst Frieda Fromm-Reichman, as described in the exquisite novel of the trials and tribulations of a severely mentally ill patient in the 1940s (*I Never Promised You a Rose Garden*), would spend lengthy sessions even when her patients were mute. *Staying* and *being* were the buzzwords for the care of the mostly nonresponsive chronically ill patients. Robert Lindner's 1950s' book *The Fifty Minute Hour: A Collection of True Psychoanalytic Tales* was a national best-seller.

As we will explore later, the 50-minute hour mostly died in the 1990s, with the last gasps of indemnity insurance (although it is now being resurrected as ever more psychiatrists are no longer willing to contract with health care insurers).

Until the advent of health care coverage for mental health in the early 1970s, experienced clinicians expected to charge more for their services than their more junior colleagues. Patients expected this, although there might be some negotiation of the hourly rate. Clinicians were free to talk about their fees with colleagues, without the current concern of violating antitrust regulations.

NONPARITY FOR MENTAL HEALTH

In the heady times of the 1960s when health care for all, or at least for seniors and the disabled, began to be considered as a right rather than a privilege, there were misgivings about how this mandate should be applied to the mentally ill. From the onset of Medicare in 1965, Congress agreed that Medicare outpatient mental health would only be covered at 50% of usual and customary charges, while other medical services from nonmental health disciplines would be covered at 80%. Inpatient psychiatric stays had lifetime limits (90 days), while such a limitation was unthinkable for other medical disciplines. Parity for mental health care was a dead issue from the onset of Medicare, as it had been with Blue Cross and other health care insurance companies.

Because of the fear of the "elastic utilization" for mental health services (more so than for other disciplines), federal and other health plans set up a number of barriers to utilization for outpatient mental health care: high co-insurance payments before insurance provided any support, and higher co-pays for each visit.

MENTAL HEALTH INSURANCE: LONGER INPATIENT STAYS AND NOW OUTPATIENT COVERAGE

In the 1970s, a surge of interest in augmenting coverage for mental health swept the nation. One after another, state legislatures mandated at least minimal outpatient and generous inpatient insurance for psychiatric and addiction treatment. In Massachusetts, for example, all health insurance was mandated to include a $500 yearly outpatient benefit as well as more liberal inpatient benefits.

Prior to the advent of mental health outpatient coverage, patients were often forced to make the decision: Shall I go on a vacation or get into treatment? Get a new overcoat or see a therapist? Before mental health insurance, payment for services came from patients' discretionary income or their more-well-to-do parents. As a result, patients might come from the middle class if single, but more often from the upper middle class if married with children. Lower-income individuals were rarely seen in private practices.

IMPLICATIONS OF WIDER MENTAL HEALTH INSURANCE COVERAGE FOR THE CLINICIAN

The mandate that all health insurance must provide at least limited mental health outpatient coverage has been wonderful for patients but at times a double-edged sword for clinicians. The good news was that with insurance coverage, access to appropriate private outpatient mental health care was greatly expanded. More patients are being seen, although typically for fewer visits per year, because of insurance company-specific limitations of the number of visits each year.

The bad news, as will be discussed later, was that clinicians have had to jump through more hoops to get those visits paid for, and to change their practice patterns to maintain income—or else opt out of the system by not accepting the arbitrary insurance fees and conditions associated with the insurance carriers.

Before outpatient mental health coverage, clinicians saw most private mental health outpatients (subsequently often referred to here as psychiatric patients) weekly or more often, often for months or years. With patients so well known to their therapists, casual process notes, not formal histories and follow-up notes, seemed appropriate and were the norm, not the exception. Psychoanalysts might see eight patients a year, with many analyses lasting four to five years. Other psychotherapists and psychiatrists might have caseloads that could range from 20 to 50, although community mental health center psychiatrists and very busy private practitioners could carry case loads from 200 to a thousand or more, with patients seen briefly and infrequently when not in crisis.

Before mental health insurance, billing and updating patients' accounts could be done by the clinician at the end of each month from home, in part of an evening. Patients would pay by return mail or at the next session in the office. Patients almost always had to pay out-of-pocket for missed appointments. Collections consistently ranged well above 90%. There were no forms to be filled out, no need for secretarial support, nor any need of a billing or collection service. It would not be unusual for psychiatrists and psychotherapists to see patients in a home office.

Initially, insurance companies merely expected some evidence of what they were paying for. They hired nurses to visit hospitals to ensure that there were documented justifications for the admission (by Diagnostic Related Group [DRG] code for Medicare patients) or for extended stays by diagnosis. At the onset of mental health coverage, because of the insurance companies' limited expenditures on outpatient mental health services, there were no documentation demands for outpatient visits.

Gradually, however, insurance companies began to require filling out complex, seemingly idiosyncratic forms. These indemnity insurance payers wanted to keep track of what their subscribers were being billed for. Within a year of the initiation of outpatient mental health insurance coverage, across the country and without ceremony or even much comment, the 50-minute hour shrank to 45 minutes. Neither patients nor clinicians noted any difference in the process of care, nor the outcome. But this decrease in the length of "the psychiatric hour" marked a beginning of a steady slide down the slippery slope.

PHASING OUT INDEMNITY INSURANCE: THE MANAGED CARE INDUSTRY IS BORN

In the 1970s and 1980s, mental health insurance charges and costs were mainly unregulated, although there were dollar or session limits to outpatient care. Mental health's share of the total health care dollar soared from 2% to 12% of health care costs. Psychiatric inpatient stays, which had been 7 days per lifetime in some cities, stretched to 30 days per admission, some policies even covering 120 days annually.

National chains built psychiatric hospitals and chemical dependency treatment units all around the country. Thirty-day "cookie cutter" inpatient drug/alcohol detoxification and rehabilitation programs were allowed and did not have to justify the medical necessity of the stay (despite a lack of evidence that inpatient care was more effective than an intensive outpatient program for alcoholism). Scandals emerged as some proprietary hospitals actually hired bounty hunters to recruit people with only marginal mental health problems to be admitted to their inpatient services.

The next evolution in health care coverage was the shift from indemnity insurance to various gradations of managed payment for health care. Indemnity insurance paid the bill, accepting the usual and customary community fee structure for inpatient admissions, procedures, and office visits. A natural consequence of the increasing liberalization of mental health benefits was the development of behavioral health benefits management companies to rein in charges that might seem excessive or fraudulent. Managed care, including the specialty of managed behavioral health care, gradually spread from California to across the nation over the next two decades. Then another barrier to ready access, the gatekeeper, was created. Many large self-insured companies required employees to visit their Employee Assistance Program before prior authorization would be granted to see an outside private therapist. Additionally, some managed care organizations (MCOs) required enrollees to visit their primary care physicians before obtaining a prior authorization to see a mental health specialist.

MANAGING ACCESS, REIMBURSEMENT RATES, AND DOCUMENTATION REQUIREMENTS

Managed care organizations (MCOs) excluded some practitioners from their in-network provider panel for a variety of reasons: too many specialists already in that geographic area, lack of board certification, not enough years in practice, or not practicing in a cost-effective manner. Others clinicians were excluded because they made too many appeals of their denials or otherwise caused administrative discomfort for the MCO. Many patients with long-standing therapeutic relationships found that their mental health clinicians were no longer "in network," and thus no longer affordable. MCOs also gradually set reimbursement rates in an idiosyncratic, sometimes draconian manner.

Finally, the MCOs began making requirements for inpatient and outpatient documentation with periodic chart audits to deny previously paid claims.

HEALTH CARE AS A PROFIT CENTER: THE CORPORATE PERSPECTIVE

Initially health insurers were mostly nonprofit service organizations with a basic pass-through mechanism: The physician submitted a bill of an insured patient, and the bill was paid according to a previously agreed upon fee schedule. But then those insurers realized that they could successfully restrict expensive care in the name of holding down consumer premiums. Rather suddenly, these nonprofit organizations were joined by for-profit entities with a vision that there was major money to be made in managing the health care dollar. Secret proprietary requirements for "medical necessity" for hospital admissions started to be used. Denials of payment for care escalated, providing an almost Kafka-esque situation. The MCOs were careful to point out that they never denied care: That was the clinician's prerogative. Rather, they maintained their right to deny payment for services that did not meet their own established criteria for medical necessity.

MCOs saw themselves as part of a publicly owned, well-capitalized industry, with service as a product, clinicians as providers, and patients as subscribers or consumers. This conceptualization, however, led to perverse incentives: Denial of care leads to increased return on the shareholders' investment. Followed to an extreme, the quick death of a chronically ill patient could be seen as a desired outcome, since the patient's costs far exceeded his or her premiums.

Health care could be seen as a commodity whose quality and quantity could be shaped by market forces. Thus, there could be limits on types and amounts of services, and provider panels could be aligned with the corporate profit goals while avoiding lawsuits and adverse publicity. No longer would "any willing provider" be allowed to participate in a panel. Even gag orders, so that clinicians could not disparage an MCO's policies, were written into some contracts. Provider fees could be gradually squeezed with little corporate consequence. With little competition among the MCOs, and their products universally in demand (except for the 43,000,000 that could not afford to purchase health insurance), MCO profits skyrocketed.

In the 1990s, MCO entrepreneurs bought out each other's firms, merged, went public, and made fortunes. One MCO CEO earned $900 million in a single year. By 1997, even if one ignores the stock options and just looks at the top five salaries of CEOs for the large publicly traded MCOs, those salaries averaged $12 million a year. Moreover, the stock-related wealth of the top 23 highest paid managed care executives could have provided health coverage for 18% of the entire population of California (Court & Smith, 1999). Currently, it is generally accepted that MCO management costs now consume about 30% of the health care dollar.

MCOs now control: access to care, which clinicians can provide that care, the amount of care provided, and the reimbursement for that care. Of interest, the American Medical Association tried its utmost in 1965 to fight off the start-up of Medicare due to fears of socialized, government-controlled medicine. Four decades later what we now have is capitalistic, corporate-controlled medicine. Most median physician salaries have not been in free fall with MCOs, but clinicians are now corporation-contracted providers of health care rather than enterprising practitioners.

HEALTH CARE AS A PROFIT CENTER: THE CLINICIAN'S PERSPECTIVE

Quite notable in the MCO era is the extensive amount of paperwork required to obtain payment for services delivered. Physicians' offices, for example, each employ personnel whose sole job is filling out forms, requesting prior authorization, and appealing denials of payment. A whole new claims-submission medical assistant job description has been spawned.

MCOs have also succeeded in delivering at times draconian cuts in reimbursement, especially it seems, for some of the cognitive (nonsurgical) services. Moreover, the MCOs have also set up incentives and disincentives for care given by downregulating fees for certain services more than others. In the context of standardization of charges, extensive Clinical Procedural Terminology (CPT) codes have been developed to describe the multiple services that clinicians provide for their patients. CPT codes dictate how much a clinician will be paid for performing a certain piece of reimbursable work.

Most people think of five-digit numbers as zip codes, like 90210 (an area in Hollywood, site of a current TV show) or 02906 (the east side of Providence, where the TV show *Providence* was filmed). But clinicians also think of five-digit numbers as reimbursement for work performed.

When clinicians in all specialties are being paid less for some of their CPT codes charges, what do they do to maintain their income? The simplest answer is: They try to do more of that which is better reimbursed, if practicable. Gastroenterologists and cardiologists, for example, discovered that they would be paid six times more per unit of time for procedures (like endoscopies and catheterizations) than for cognitive services (talking with the patient).

IMPACT OF MANAGED CARE ON PSYCHIATRISTS AND PSYCHOTHERAPISTS

Initially mental health clinicians weathered the introduction of indemnity mental health insurance with minimal changes in practice style, except that the 50-minute hour changed to the 45-minute hour.

As coverage for outpatient coverage expanded, management of that care also expanded (even though that management at times cost more than its projected savings). Managed care companies began to insist on the right to audit inpatient and outpatient chart notes, requiring documentation of the beginning and ending time of each session, each page being signed, and so forth. Documentation of the number of "elements" in the present illness or the mental status evaluation began to be required in order to get fair compensation for work done, in case of retrospective audit. Detailed summaries were required for extension of outpatient sessions after an initial six sessions, as well as documentation about progress made, disabilities and symptoms present, and the likelihood of improvement.

Denial of payment had little *corporate* consequences.

In addition to greatly increased documentation requirements in ordinary charts and the innumerable questionnaires and billing forms, there were huge changes in reimbursement by CPT code for the clinicians' cognitive services.

Unfortunately, mental health clinicians have no high-paying procedures. There are no CPT codes for a "grief-otomy," "super-ego-pexy," or "ego transplant." Mental health clinicians' "unit of commerce" is not cataract extraction (which can be done much more quickly now than it was 10 years ago, yet with hardly a decline in the fee for the procedure). Rather, the mental health's unit of commerce is really *time*, which is not distensible.

Not being able to find more hours in the day, psychiatrists discovered that they had to change their practice patterns if they were to maintain their income from outpatient practice. In the latter part of the 1990s, most psychiatrists still accepting insurance for private outpatient practices began to decrease time slots allocated for psychotherapy in favor of time slots allocated for medication management, referring out their psychotherapy components of care to nonpsychiatric clinicians.

A sea change had occurred for psychiatrists' locus of control. The therapist-patient dyad morphed into a triangular relationship. The clinician was no longer an independent professional, but was now under contract with one or several MCOs.

THE 50-MINUTE HOUR, A CASUALTY OF MANAGED CARE

From the onset of mental health insurance reimbursement, psychiatry had a special niche, so-called CPT G codes, or CPT time codes. All the common outpatient service codes for mental health were associated with a given number of minutes. Outpatient charges supposedly reflected "face time" of patient and therapist. There were also G codes for family therapy, couple therapy, and group therapy. G codes also reflected time spent for the initial psychiatric evaluation session.

But with the publication of the 1998 CPT Code Book, everything changed.

Table 1 Blue Cross of Rhode Island Psychiatry/MD Fee Schedule
for Commercial Products Effective April 1, 2007

Code	Description	Fee/Time	Fee/Minute
Office			
90801	Psy dx interview	$171.51/60	$2.86
90805	Psytx, off, 20–30 min w/E&M	70.75/20	3.54
90806	Psytx, off, 45–50 min	106.72/45	2.37
90807	Psyx, off, 45–50 w/E&M	117.68/45	2.61
90862	Medication management	58.18/15	3.88
Hospital			
92222	Initial hospital day	122.00/50	2.44
99231	Subsequent hospital day	60.00/15	4.00
99232	Subsequent hospital day	60.08/25	2.40
99239	Hospital discharge day	104.16/30	3.42

Managed care companies began using differential reimbursement schedules (CPT codes) for 15-minute visits, 30-minute visits,
50-minute visits, and so on (Table 1). Also, there were differential
incentives for doing medication management or medication management with psychotherapy rather than just psychotherapy alone.
Another disincentive for psychiatrists doing only psychotherapy:
MCOs put no limits on medication management sessions per year,
while some put limits on the number of psychotherapy sessions
allowed without subsequent tedious prior authorization forms.

For the first time, there was a marked discrepancy between
reimbursement for psychotherapy with medication (90807), a 20- to
30-minute time code, and a new code, medication management
(90862), without a time requirement. Without warning, psychotherapy codes were reimbursed 30–50% less *per minute*.

Additionally, in order to be paid in full, certain elements were
required to be documented in various parts of the workup, including
up to 6 to 13 elements in the mental status. By contrast, the med
management code, 90862, often was reimbursed at almost twice as
much per minute, had no limitations of number of visits, and had
far fewer documentation requirements.

Allowable charges per minute for psychiatric CPT outpatient
codes varied considerably from state to state, with some states having rates 20–30% higher than their neighbors. Of note, 90862,

medication management, with very few documentation requirements in comparison to the evaluation with medication management and psychotherapy codes, produces higher reimbursement
(per minute), and is 50% greater per minute than 90807. What
psychiatrists had been doing the most of, 90807, suddenly was
being undervalued, or, at the very least, relatively underpaid.

THE NEW PSYCHIATRY

There is an adage in medicine that health care economists use: "Care
follows the dollar." There is another adage that mental health advo-
cates use: "Dollars should follow the patient." With this CPT-induced
sea change, both have happened. The 50-minute hour (90807), or
more correctly, the 45-minute hour, has become a casualty of the shift
from psychiatry's having a unique position (and G codes) to being
just another medical specialty under tight managed care control.
One good outcome of MCOs' tight rein on costs of mental health
care is that actuaries now predict that when mental health parity
becomes the law of the land in 2010, the per-member-per-month
premium will only increase by about 0.5%.

The MCOs' prioritization (through financial incentives and disincentives) of medication management (90862) has greatly increased
mental health access for sick psychiatric patients of modest means:
These insured patients are being seen, and seen more promptly.
Moreover, those psychiatrists accepting insurance have been able
to maintain their incomes (actually psychiatrists' incomes have
recently been going up slightly). But the price that psychiatrists
have had to pay is the surrender of what was familiar, comfortable,
and demonstrably effective.

Thus was born the 20-minute hour, or sometimes the 15-minute
hour. Currently, though, many other mental health clinicians still
have their 45–50 minutes of face time for psychotherapy. How long
will that luxury be allowed to continue?

Hence this primer: an effort to make the most of the face time
allotted to each individual patient's care. This primer is designed
for both the clinician that wants to continue to do some therapy
along with medication management and the therapist that wants to
use face time as efficiently and effectively as possible. Some of the
shortcuts suggested here should certainly help out.

REFLECTING ON THE IMPACT OF
MANAGED BEHAVIORAL HEALTH CARE

Has managed behavioral health care been bad? It depends on whom you ask, and when you ask it. As inferred, older established psychiatrists bemoan the passing of the 50-minute hour: a leisurely pace and adequate compensation with fascinating work. They are sad to lose the opportunity of doing intensive psychotherapy—that activity now being referred out to psychologists and master's prepared social workers, that are, no surprise, paid by the MCOs at a lower rate than psychiatrists for a designated block of time.

But from a public health perspective, over the past decade several changes in mental health have been good. The number of patients in treatment has more than quadrupled in the past decade, with four times as many patients on antidepressants now than in 1988. The suicide rate has not increased. Fewer patients are in acute psychiatric care beds at one time than in past decades.

Two major goals have been accomplished: (1) Access to mental health care has been greatly increased, and (2) cost of overall mental health services (inpatient and outpatient combined) has decreased. Decades ago, inpatient care (for general medicine as well as psychiatry and the addictions) was consuming a disproportionate share of the health dollar without providing apparent added value. The increased scrutiny of hospital stays for medical necessity produced decreased lengths of stay (LOS).

UNINTENDED OUTCOMES OF MANAGED CARE

Any major policy shift on a nationwide basis will have intended as well as unintended consequences, the latter often unpredicted. An unintended consequence of the Jackson Hole Group (theoreticians and national health services leaders), who early on encouraged the development of managed care, has been a huge increase in the administrative costs for the entire health care system. Moreover, rather than competition on quality measures among the MCOs, there has been consolidation into publicly traded MCOs. In true capitalistic fashion, MCOs have focused on return on investment (ROI) more than quality of care.

To deal with the increasing burden of paperwork to input patients into the system and collect for work performed, practicing physicians, clinics, and hospitals have also had to augment their office staff to do the telephone work of prior authorizations and claims submission. For psychiatry, this greatly decreased profits for psychiatric hospitals and drove many proprietary hospitals into bankruptcy, or else they morphed into nursing homes or residential treatment centers for adolescents. Thus, an unintended consequence of closely monitored utilization of services: Currently there is a shortage of acute psychiatric hospital beds in many parts of the nation.

So where is the outrage about managed care? Physicians are angry about the abuses they have suffered from MCOs but feel powerless. Consumers are usually not upset about managed care, only about their increasing premiums, which are seen as primarily related to the increased costs of new technologies and medications. Employers are upset only about the rising costs of their employee benefits, so they often switch MCOs and pass more of the costs of health care onto their employees. And mental health clinicians are not talking much about the 800-pound gorilla. Rather, they are trying to adapt as quickly as they can to the new 20-minute hour, something that few in practice now experience in their training.

Surprisingly, public policy debates at a national level have rarely addressed the lack of added health value associated with the 30% costs of regulating and administering the health care system. Perhaps at some point, managed care was a "necessary evil" to correct problems in the system. But now it seems time to move on, although the insurance company lobbyists would not like us to think that. The single-payer system, staunchly advocated by Jim McDonald, MD, of Seattle, the only psychiatrist in Congress, died a quiet death almost a decade ago. Perhaps the current unexpected alliance of Wal-Mart and a large labor union on the need for a national policy on universal health care coverage, plus the election of Senator Barack Obama as president of the United States, will be auspicious for much needed change.

CONCLUSION

This primer assumes the reader is knowledgeable about the intricacies of psychotherapies and, for prescribers, psychopharmacology. Hence, the focus of this primer is on how to make efficient use of the precious little time allotted to seeing the patient, typically now 20 minutes or less of face-to-face time with the patient.

This book is based on the author's experience as a:

Psychiatrist in an academic outpatient private practice (thirty years)
Staff psychiatrist at a community mental health center (three years)
Supervisor in a residency medication management clinic (four years)

The author wishes to acknowledge a debt to the late Pietro Castelnovo-Tedesco, a UCLA- and University of Tennessee-based psychoanalyst. His groundbreaking book, *The Twenty-Minute Hour*, was published in 1965 for primary care physicians, and focused on what therapeutic issues could be addressed in as few as 20-minute sessions, and how to do it. Twenty-minute sessions seemed to be an appropriate amount of time to engage with the patient and deal with some psychodynamic issues. His goal was that some internists would learn to fit psychotherapy into their generalist practices in an amount of time that they would probably be willing to devote to this task. His book came out at a time when the fee for such a visit varied between $5 and $15, depending upon the practice's location. Castelnovo-Tedesco's book was reissued in paperback by APPI Press without revision, but with a revised preface, in 1986.

It seems timely now that the subject of the 20-minute hour be readdressed, this time to deal with some practical issues in working with patients for the mental health clinician in the 21st century.

At a simplistic level, 20 minutes can be enough time to say: "Hello," "I'm glad to see you," "What's going on?" "How do you understand that?" "What needs to be done?" "What are our goals?" "When shall we meet again?" and "Good-bye." In that context, a lot of dynamic, cognitive behavioral, or interpersonal therapy can be accomplished, with medication adjustment done as need be.

Part I

Ways to Make the 20-Minute Hour Work for You

Many clinicians currently in practice were trained using the 50-minute hour with long-term psychotherapy patients. They were allowed the time to investigate negative transference, which at times could allow for major psychological breakthroughs; for example, a writer's block could be linked to feelings about the father's death.

Today's clinician, however, is allowed far less time, so efforts now need to be expended in fostering positive transference, applying cognitive behavioral and supportive techniques, plus disease management and psychoeducation. In this primer, we use the term *20-minute hour* to stand for whatever short span is allocated to see a patient, write a note, at times talk to a supervisor or colleague, and then get ready for the next patient on a nonstop daily schedule.

The 20-minute hour allows for brief psychotherapy to be added to, if appropriate, checking on the patient's medication status. Sometimes these sessions, for prescribers, are called med checks, but so much more than checking on medications can be accomplished: the medication component of the visit usually being the quick and easy part.

A useful mnemonic (modified from H. Steven Moffic, MD) for med check is:

M: Medication and mood
E: Environmental changes (home life, job, family, or other relationships)
D: Diagnosis (because after a few sessions, more Axis I and Axis II diagnoses often become evident)
C: Coordination of care (since many patients are also cared for by other providers)

H: Handouts (about medications, cognitive behavioral therapy [CBT], other resources, or for homework)

E: Empathy, such an important part of history taking and throughout, especially when the patient speaks of a great loss

C: Cost of care or co-pays for medication, which can be burdensome for some

K: Knowledge base for the patient, which needs to be ever expanded as part of disease management, and self-control. It is important to make sure that the patient gets the take-home message by asking the patient to reiterate, for example, the medication dosage and the therapy homework to make sure that he or she understands and then remembers what should be expected.

Chapter 1

Beginnings—Not a Moment to Spare

WHAT TO EXPECT

Patients that are referred to mental health professionals for evaluation and treatment are special. Since 80% of the psychiatric care in the United States is *not* rendered by mental health specialists, your patient may well have one or more of the following characteristics:

The patient is informed enough to know that specialist care will often provide better results than nonspecialist care.

The patient is not bothered by the stigma of seeing a mental health clinician.

The patient has failed to respond to a primary care physician's initial attempts at treating psychiatric symptoms, or the primary care physician may not feel comfortable using psychotropic medications.

The patient has an overdue co-pay balance or in other ways may feel unwelcome or uncomfortable receiving care from his or her primary care physician.

The patient has been referred by a psychotherapist who recognizes a need for medication management to enhance (or allow) the patient's ongoing psychotherapy to proceed.

As one is thinking about the patient before he or she is seen, it may *not* be crucial at the very onset to know exactly why the patient has decided to see a mental health specialist rather than just a primary care physician (PCP), as opposed to some other helping professional. After all, this may not be at all on the patient's primary agenda, and the information will come out soon enough. But it is important to be aware that patients referred to a mental health specialist typically are more likely to be complicated from the perspective of severity of illness, chronicity, and co-morbidity. The question of "Why now?" however, must be addressed early on.

HOW TO PREPARE FOR EACH VISIT

Although some clinicians prefer to read the chart before ever setting eyes on the patient, others prefer to review whatever information is available *with* the patient, so if there are inaccuracies, since the patient is the world's expert on himself or herself, the patient is given an immediate opportunity of making sure the clinician "gets it right." Moreover, many managed behavioral health organizations insist on only paying for "face time," and not for preparation for a visit, filling out forms for the patient outside the session, and so forth.

Before the clinician ventures to the waiting room to meet the new patient, there are certain items in the office that will facilitate patient "throughput" (efficiency of care). The following items are useful, and many can be carried in a briefcase (see Table 1.1).

THE INITIAL ENCOUNTER

Venturing into the busy clinic waiting room, one can often pick out which is the new patient based on sex, age, race, and brief information about the patient's occupation from just glancing at the face sheet of the chart. To preserve the patient's anonymity, it may be preferable to call the patient by his or her first name, and if there is recognition, make an introduction with a handshake, walking to the office with the patient. (Later, the issue of how the patient wishes to be addressed in the future needs to be discussed.)

If the hallway going to the office is narrow, one can motion the patient to walk ahead with a simple set of instructions ("It's the first office on the right after the red fire extinguisher.") This provides a very brief partial mental status exam, with an opportunity to study physical attributes as well as the patient's ability to orient and gait. If the hallway to the office is long and wide, while walking alongside the patient, one can casually indicate what will transpire in the office over the next 45 minutes without fear of compromising any confidentiality and one can even engage in minor neutral type of chitchat.

Table 1.1 Office Supplies for the Initial Interview

1.	Kleenex
2.	DSM-IV, the smaller ring-bound copy
3.	Patient's chart and billing form
4.	Isagel (a simple way for hand sanitation after shaking hands when the patient enters or leaves the office)
5.	Pad of lined paper for note taking and two pens or a computer
6.	Yellow highlighter pen to indicate in the write-up important blanks in the initial workup that still need to be filled in
7.	Smaller notepad with just the clinician's name on it (for writing excuses from work, to whom it may concern, etc.)
8.	Calling cards/appointment cards
9.	Clipboard and nondescript ballpoint pen for forms for patient's use
10.	Release of information forms allowing correlative information from other therapists or family members
11.	Handouts about the patient's responsibilities in the treatment setting (the contract), medications' specific side effects, sources for purchase of light boxes for seasonal affective disorder
12.	A demonstration copy of David Burns, MD's, *Feeling Good* or Rob Wilson and Rhena Branch's *Cognitive Behavioural Therapy for Dummies*
13.	"Do Not Disturb" sign for office door
14.	Readily visible clock previously synchronized with wristwatch
15.	Prescription pad, for prescribers
16.	PC with a connection to ePocrates.com online (with colored pictures of various medications) for prescribers
17.	Telephone on the "Do Not Disturb" mode

When in the waiting room and then in the office, the development of a comfortable but somewhat standardized manner of introducing oneself to the patient will be quite useful, since then the patient's response to the known stimulus gives the clinician valuable initial information.

After the patient is settled down in the relatively uncluttered and quiet office, one may wish to use an opening gambit such as:

> Here's what I know about you, from what's in the chart. I have to read selected parts of it myself, so I might as well read it out loud. I want you to have an active role in this process, since you are the world's expert on you. I think together we'll be able to construct a good history about what the problem is. If some of the information I have here is wrong, or you don't understand, please let me know.

But first let's start with the easy stuff as I write my notes [or enter them into the computer]. Now what is the date today? How old are you? Married? Who currently is living in your household? What type of work are you doing? [Or alternatively, "What was your favorite job when you were gainfully employed?"] Where does your financial support come from? Is it enough for you to get by from month to month?

This seemingly routine information allows the clinician to begin an interview gathering simple and often straightforward information in an empathic manner. If there are painful areas of stress in the realms of living, loving, or working, that information may come popping right out. This leads to an easy transition to the history of the present illness (if it hasn't already started to emerge) and an understanding of what the patient does in a typical day.

SETTING THE STAGE

With the patient talking readily about relatively neutral items, he or she is primed to begin talking about the reason for seeking a psychiatric consultation, and the clinician is able to put some of the information about the patient's illness into the context of the patient's living situation.

The use of a semistructured interview (but always flexibly following the patient's lead) is helpful. An outline (or "cheat sheet") ensures that no important categories are left out, such as substance use and physical-sexual abuse (even when there do not seem to be any clinical cues from taking the history that those areas might be productive). Table 1.2 is an example of one such sample form. Its use will help the clinician to keep focused as well as comprehensive.

FACILITATING THE FLOW OF INFORMATION

Patients who are comfortable, nonhurried, mostly uninterrupted, and given time to answer questions thoughtfully tend to give the best histories. A minority of patients, however, are quite adept at gratuitous, tangential comments that, although interesting, are not on target. If this seems to be the patient's consistent style, a gentle

Table 1.2 Guideline for the Initial Evaluation

Name and date (plus patient file no. and date of birth if not otherwise there)

Referral source (and telephone number)

Socioeconomic, employment, cultural, and marital status

Chief complaint

History of the present illness: Current and past psychiatric treatment episodes, hospitalizations, suicide attempts

Medications, including daily doses; other meds, OTCs, and herbals

Compliance with taking of meds and with appointments

Drug/alcohol: Personal, familial, including treatments tried

Family history of mental illness

Important psychosocial information:

    Insurance/disability status

    Poverty level: Ability to meet co-pays, food stamps, housing

    Educational level/current job/others in home and their status

Physical assessment

    Allergies

    Chronic medical disorders and relevant major operations

    Pain

    Nonpsychiatric and psychiatric medications

    Obesity/body mass index and treatments tried

Mental status examination (the number of elements in MSE may determine payment)

Diagnoses on five axes

Plan: Safety issues, meds, labs, types of psychotherapy suggested or given

reminder is usually appreciated, or at least well tolerated, by most such patients. For example, "It's going to be important to focus on just a few issues during our limited time."

If the patient needs prompting about being concise, one can rest assured that he or she has heard that many times before.

Comfort and rapport during the interview are assisted by facilitative statements such as:

"Let me hear more about that."
"What else was going on during that difficult time?"
"My word, what a terrible tragedy!"

The "gosh, gee whiz" approach shows the clinician is listening with accurate empathy.

Always one is listening for sources of friction and dissatisfaction from family, job, friends, and bodily parts, as well as a sense of who is responsible for the patient's plight.

In taking a history, one should *always* assume that the patient is sexually active. One should always routinely ask if the individual has a past history of physical, sexual, or emotional abuse even if there is no suspicion leading to this in the clinical history. Moreover, with substance abuse involving more than a quarter of the population at some point in their lives, one should *always* inquire about this. In addition, one should assume that there are a variety of medical and psychiatric Axis I or Axis II co-morbidities.

Patients will usually start the present illness with the first time they presented for *treatment*, but it is equally important to know when was the first time they ever had the *symptoms* for which they now seek treatment, as well as the first time the illness was adequately *diagnosed*. Be aware that patients usually do not proffer information on co-morbid conditions, especially symptoms of mild–moderate hypomania or severe irritability.

History taking with a patient is a collaborative and often iterative process, requiring going over the present illness several times to acquire information about precipitants, accompanying suicide ideation or attempts, hospitalizations, and the all-important "Why now?" and "How are you right now?"

Patients rarely themselves rate the severity of sequential episodes, whereas it is important for the clinician to know whether or not there is a crescendo pattern of increasingly severe episodes. Rating the severity of the patient's illness will be discussed in detail in Chapter 2.

Family histories often have some neglected components. A thumbnail sketch of the patient's rearing is often useful, especially early history of physical or sexual abuse and neglect. Moreover, the genetic family history often needs some priming or prodding. It is not sufficient to ask if there is a family history of mental or substance abuse disorders. Patients often need gentle prompting here, so it is useful to say: "Do you have any parents, grandparents, aunts, uncles, cousins, nieces, nephews, or children with mental disorders? With alcohol or drug disorders? Is there anyone in the family that is nervous, had a suicide attempt? Drinks too heavily?"

Being redundant is a very useful way to tap into this information, which is usually not stored as actively available, so a little jogging of the memory can be useful.

For prescribers, melding a genetic family history into a *pharmacogenetic* history is also key, as a history of drug failures *and* successes in blood relatives gives one somewhat of an advantage in choosing which drugs to use and which to avoid. Such thorough questioning provides the patient with an understanding that such information may be more important than the patient himself or herself had considered, and also gives the patient more time to bring back to awareness this valuable information, which may inform treatment decisions.

BUILDING AND MAINTAINING A THERAPEUTIC ALLIANCE

The therapeutic alliance is the single most important part of the work of the initial intake and the subsequent 20-minute hour. A patient without a strong therapeutic alliance will probably not stay in treatment. Studies show that up to 50% of patients drop out before the fourth session. If the patient does stay in treatment, but without a strong therapeutic alliance, the likelihood of complete and appropriate adherence to the prescribed therapeutic regimen (medication or cognitive behavioral therapy (CBT) homework, or both) is diminished. Moreover, without a strong therapeutic alliance, the ever-helpful placebo response is less likely to kick in.

In this primer, we have specifically used the term *20-minute hour* rather than *15-minute med check*, because all too often a hurried visit, with four patients to be seen in the course of an hour, can cause problems in the formation of the patient's positive regard for the clinician, and in the clinician's having a satisfactory clinical experience. A survey of private practice psychiatrists in Manhattan within the past decade (when the 50-minute hour shifted to 15-minute med checks) indicated that 70% would not recommend that graduating residents go into private practice of psychiatry (while accepting insurance).

However, if there is present a multidisciplinary team to pick up the pieces in case of an emergency, and if there are a few "did not keep appointments" (DNKAs), then the clinician may be able to have satisfying work spending less than 25 minutes per patient seen. The "experienced," stable patient just needing a lithium level checked and one prescription refilled, or an attention-deficit hyperactivity disorder (ADHD) patient just needing a stimulant medication refilled, can often be comfortably seen in 15 minutes or less. But working with most patients, having to rush through the "perfunctories" leaves little time for:

1. Empathic consideration
2. Communicating with other members of the care team (psychotherapist or PCP)
3. Dealing with the unpredictable crises that overwhelm the patient's coping skills

In addition to checking on side effects of medication, the clinician needs to spend some time on regathering information on adherence to the program, as a surprisingly high proportion of patients either do not take prescribed medication as often as indicated, or may mix their prescribed medications with over-the-counter (OTC) medications, herbals, street drugs, or alcohol that can compromise progress in one way or another.

NURTURING THE THERAPEUTIC ALLIANCE

A conversational style, with natural inflections of voice and gestures, that allows time to be devoted to discussing options/preferences, and answering questions are extraordinarily important. Time is also needed for the nurturance of positive transference (and not interpreting it). But if negative transference emerges, it is important not to ignore it. It often is important to acknowledge the validity of the patient's angry feelings, to attempt to understand the clinician's role (if any) in inducing the conflict, and apologizing (if this is appropriate), to offer solutions to improve the situation, and to reassure the patient that working through the problem will serve to strengthen the therapeutic alliance.

Allowing the patient an opportunity to talk about painful matters is also an important part of nurturing the therapeutic alliance. The artistry here is not focusing on matters that are too painful for the patient to address at the moment. Sometimes gradually nibbling away at small matters will allow time for "the big one" to be addressed later on, as it is whittled down to a manageable size.

Enhancing the patient's self-esteem is another component of nurturing the therapeutic alliance. Most patients start out not feeling good about themselves, so it is a good strategy to try to bolster self-esteem. Positive comments, acknowledgment, and compliments, when appropriate, do help.

STRENGTHENING COPING MECHANISMS

The clinician acts as a role model, showing ways to use mature ego defense mechanisms such as sublimation, humor, and isolating or intellectualizing affect, among others. Instruction about self-soothing, relaxation, and learning how to placate and reward is helpful in assisting patients. The clinician acts as coach, advocate and mentor, with suggestions on how to deal with specific situations.

RESEARCH STUDIES ABOUT THE THERAPEUTIC RELATIONSHIP

Myriad studies of the effectiveness of psychotherapy point to the following factors as the essential nonspecific ingredients of a therapeutic alliance regardless of the type of psychotherapy practiced:

Genuineness/authenticity
Nonpossessive warmth
Accurate empathy
Acceptance
Supportive stance
Curiosity

At the onset, even before getting down to the business of taking a formal history, it is often important to touch on a common chord if there is an easy and natural opportunity. For the patient wearing a New England Patriots jersey with "Tom Brady" and "12" on it, talking about the recent football game (as long as you are up on it) is a good way to ease into taking a history, and also learning if the patient could concentrate enough to watch the game. With the female patient with her name on a necklace, noticing it in a positive way could be a manner of indicating that you have noticed that the patient doesn't want to get lost in the crowd. For the patient who mentions that he or she used to be a weight lifter, asking how many pounds he or she can bench-press and jerk is a way of showing personal interest.

Psychotherapy in the 20-minute hour is unlike long-term intensive, insight-oriented psychotherapy. In long-term dynamic work, supervisors often suggest the clinician take a neutral stance and maintain considerable anonymity to help foster the development of a transference neurosis. But prescribers doing medication management only have time to do small amounts of supportive psychotherapy and some snippets of cognitive behavioral therapy.

In summary, it is important to develop positive transference quickly. In each part of the diagnostic processes, as well as with follow-up visits, the clinician needs to actively consider how to foster the clinician-patient alliance, to build rapport. The goal is to become goal congruent with the patient's expressed need and to make sure "the customer gets what he or she came for."

When patients have options, they will want to return to see the clinician that shows them nonpossessive warmth, accurate empathy, and personal interest in them, rather than just their disorder. Dropping out, with DNKAs or cancellations left on the answering machine without explanation, is a common way for patients to "vote with their feet." This makes successful transition of care to another provider more difficult, and prevents the development of contingency plans in case of relapse.

MAKING THE DIAGNOSIS

By far the most frequent reason now for patients to get into treatment in most clinical settings for adult patients is some form of depression, by itself or added on to other disorders. Thus, the clinician must rapidly sort out the seriousness of the depression: For example, is it a major depression, a dysthymia, an adjustment disorder, a depression associated with a medical disorder, or a depression as part of a bipolar disorder? Treatment or referral for each is quite different, and delaying "getting it right" puts adequate treatment in some peril.

All clinicians are familiar with the mechanics of making a psychiatric diagnosis. The most important diagnosis to be on top of is major depressive episode, which fortunately has a great mnemonic: SIGECAPS (sleep, interest, guilt, energy, concentration, appetite for food and sex, psychomotor retardation or agitation, and suicide).

Other useful mnemonics (for those so disposed) include DIGFAST for mania (distractible, insomnia, grandiose, flight of ideas, activities, speed, and thoughtlessness), thanks to Dr. Ghaemi. For bipolar depression, Dr. Pies has devised WHIPLASHED as an aid in diagnosis: worse or wired when taking antidepressants; hypomanic or hyperthymic temperament; irritable, hostile, or mixed features when depressed; psychomotor retardation more common in bipolar I and less common in bipolar II, where agitation is more likely; loaded family history of mood swings or affective illness; abrupt onset or termination of depressive bouts or episodes lasting less than three months; seasonal or postpartum depressions, depressed in the winter and hypomanic in the spring; hyperphagia and hypersomnia in depression; early onset, with major depression before age 25, especially with psychotic features; and delusions, hallucinations, or other psychotic features more common in bipolar than unipolar depression.

And for psychosocial factors there is "family and friends with a WISE HALO" (work, income, social environment, education, housing, access to health care services, legal, and other) thanks to Dr. Madaan. For most major disorders, the clinician is well advised to make use of the *Diagnostic and Statistical Manual of Mental Disorders* (DSM-IV) to make sure that a diagnosis made meets all formal criteria. (See the appendix for Chapter 1, page 197, for other useful mnemonics.)

Textbooks describe disorders, while the patient's *illness* occurs uniquely in the way that he or she experiences it. Thus, the patient's DSM-IV psychiatric disorder must be understood in terms of the psychosocial milieu and intrapsychic issues in order to really understand what is common and what is special about the patient and his or her plight.

Rather than making the diagnosis *on* the patient, one should consider making the diagnosis *with* the patient. For example, when the clinician is trying to confirm a diagnosis, one can readily show the patient the small DSM-IV ring-bound book, including the front cover, saying: "This is a copy of the American Psychiatric Association's handbook for psychiatric diagnoses. Let's see if the description of your difficulties with _____ would fit with the criteria in this book."

At times, however, with the less educated patient, it may be best to read a loosely paraphrased text.

This technique is very well received by a vast majority of nonpsychotic patients with a variety of disorders, including paranoid personality, borderline personality, obsessive-compulsive personality, hypomania, generalized anxiety, social phobia, panic disorder, as well as kleptomania, intermittent explosive disorder, and the addictive disorders. However, for patients with intelligence considerably below average, it is best to simplify many of the two- and three-syllable terms in DSM-IV.

Patients appreciate playing an active role in the diagnostic process, being able to hear the full range of criteria, and being able to see where they fit into the scheme of things. The patient's realization that he or she is not unique is a powerful aid to healing.

CONCLUDING THE INITIAL ASSESSMENT

After all the information has been gathered, the clinician needs to formulate a plan for action, which for the prescriber usually will include writing a prescription for some psychoactive medication. Given that all the antidepressants, mood stabilizers, and atypical antipsychotic agents in current use are, in their class, about equally potent, the choice of medication comes down to co-payment cost, potential side effects, and patient preferences. Sexual side effects and weight gain are clearly the most feared side effects. The common serious adverse effects must also be presented to the patient so that he or she can make an informed choice.

Pharmacogenetic information, as mentioned, also can be very helpful in the decision making, as well as the patient's prior medication record. Patient preferences, even if based on a "series of one," such as how the neighbor fared on that same drug, or other information gleaned from TV ads or Internet searches, have to be given due weight in the outcome, with the prescriber's reasoning made appropriately clear.

Collaborative care becomes an important part in adherence to any regimen. Since there are two dozen antidepressants, five frequently used atypical antipsychotics, five effective mood stabilizers, and an equal number of anxiolytics, the choice of which medication to choose, from within classes, should often be a joint one. Again, the important principle is that the patient is participating in the treatment process.

As the appointment winds down, it is important to say to the patient: "I've asked you a lot of questions, so now it's your turn to ask me any questions that you need to."

This rarely takes much time. The patient who has been very alert and involved is usually quite tired by this time, so only the most pressing issues come out, and such an open-ended question invariably saves time in the long term.

Before writing out the prescription, the prescriber needs to be certain to inform the patient of the risks, benefits, and alternatives of the medication choice, and record that "R/B/A" has been performed. It is probably best to write in the chart a statement such as:

> The risks of _____ and benefits of this medication have been carefully explained to the patient, and I feel that he/she is making an informed choice in accepting it.

In the context of prescribing medication, it is a mistake not to assume that any female is sexually active. Indeed, according to the advice of many leading journal articles on medicating female patients, one should inquire of all female patients *over the age of 9* about their method of contraception, since there is some increased risk to a fetus from many psychoactive medications (especially Depakote) even before the patient knows that she is pregnant.

Many patients are leery about taking any psychoactive medication. One can say to such a patient:

> Side effects other than what we have discussed are possible, though not likely. I suggest you keep the package insert and, if you are having some symptoms, read it. If you are really worried, of course you can call my answering machine and I will get back to you.

It is often helpful to tell the patient:

> There is no medication in the world that I can prescribe for you that will not be hurtful to someone. Aspirin resulted in 41 deaths last year. But the risks for this medication are rather small, and we will be observing for any adverse reactions as well as ordinary side effects.

Setting the time for the next appointment and (the ceremony of) handing the patient the prescription terminate the interview.

TIME MANAGEMENT

In grappling with all the clinical information from the initial interview, the clinician readily realizes that there is not a moment to lose in the allotted time for the initial workup. Typically, 60 minutes will be scheduled to complete the intake process. But because of paperwork, it is often best to spend only 45–50 minutes face time with the patient. Obviously, if charting can all be completed in the patient's presence, there can be more face time. No other appointment with the patient is as likely to run over the allotted time as the initial appointment.

Sometimes not all mandated areas on the semistructured interview can be covered, especially if the patient is tangential, hard of hearing, or has a complex and lengthy past history of relevant psychiatric care, medication trials, hospitalizations, and failed therapists. For such patients, it is best to remind the patient that the evaluation will be continued next time. The clinician may wish to use a yellow highlighter to indicate in the chart areas that typically would have been covered in an initial evaluation were it not for time constraints. Highlighting cuts down on errors of omission that otherwise might be missed on the patient's first follow-up visit. Before managed care pressures, outpatient evaluations used to take three to six sessions and inpatient evaluations (at McLean) would often take six weeks.

Despite the frustration of trying to cover all the bases in 45 or so minutes, this is still the longest uninterrupted time the clinician may ever spend with the patient, so it is best to make certain that the experience is a positive one for the patient.

Should the patient arrive on time, be 25 years of age, never having had a depression before; should the patient have no Axis II personality disorders; should the patient come from a stable family with no psychiatric or substance use issues; should there be no overwhelming story of sexual abuse or maternal neglect; should the patient be intelligent and highly motivated; and should the patient have only a few brief questions to ask, then taking and recording an initial psychiatric evaluation is often easily accomplished in less than the allotted time. At the community mental health center's acute care outpatient clinic, where I worked for three years, we might see one such intake a month. But for the other 39 intakes, there is far greater complexity. In private practice settings, one is usually able to complete the initial assessment and its recording readily within 60 minutes. But whatever the setting, the actual assessment *process* may require not only the initial 60-minute time block, but also several other shorter sessions before the clinician can comfortably put together all the DSM-IV axes and the basic dynamics of the case.

Chapter 2

Measuring Symptoms

The busy clinician needs to know as soon as possible, and as accurately as possible, information about the key indicators of a patient's condition. For example, in the emergency room, when a patient comes in after a suicide attempt, it would be important to know whether or not the patient's current episode of life-threatening behaviors is part of a crescendo trajectory, as this has ramifications for patient management and even safety. Just how bad does the patient think his or her illness is right now? Often words will fail to do justice to the patient's experience. Moreover, *mild, moderate*, and *severe* often don't contain adequate nuance for treatment decisions. Business schools have a mantra: "If you can't measure it, you can't manage it." This also applies to clinicians working with their patients. But the task is how to measure it meaningfully *and* quickly.

In order to assess rapidly the patient's current state, clinicians over the years have relied on a variety of measuring tools. Some researchers tend to use Aaron Beck's scales for depression, anxiety, and hopelessness. Other researchers use one of the multiple scales published four decades ago by Max Hamilton, MD. More recent short scales by John Rush, MD, and others seem to be an improvement. But few clinicians in nonresearch settings use such tools, because of time pressures. What every clinician needs are some accurate shortcuts, to rapidly unveil the patient's clinical condition.

USING A VISUAL ANALOGUE SCALE TO ASSESS PATIENTS' PERCEPTION OF THEIR INTERIOR STATE

Simple digits, on a 0 to 10 scale to rate how a patient is feeling, can be used without difficulty as a self-rating scale for various aspects of psychopathology by patients with IQs ranging from 60 to 200. Such a technique in clinical practice does show stability when there is no change in the clinical condition, and when the clinical condition changes, the numbers also change as anticipated. Both the initial self-rating and subsequent changes appear to have good face validity.

Drawing a 100 mm line on a sheet of paper and asking a patient to rate some aspect of his or her condition with a single vertical mark is an old technique (many cigarettes are 100 mm long). More recently, the Joint Commission on Accreditation of Health Care Organizations (JCAHO) has required all hospitalized patients be rated at intake for their pain by means of a visual analogue scale. The mandated pain scale shows faces with changing expressions as the pain increases from 0 (a smiley face) to 10 (a very sad face showing copious tears). This technique was pioneered by Jimmie Holland, MD, formerly director of the Psychiatric Consultation Service at Sloan Kettering Memorial Hospital for Cancer in New York City.

With the visually aided pain scale as a model, I came up with an adapted version for depression. This depression scale has now been used by clinicians for a number of years and has been found to be very quick and useful. This visual analogue scale makes sense immediately to both patients and clinicians. Only a cursory explanation of how to use it has ever been necessary. It is a very rapid way to "get to the bottom line."

The clinician shows the Visual Analogue Depression Scale (Figure 2.1) to the patient and then says: "On a scale from –10 to 0, when –10 is as much sadness or depression as anyone can bear, and 0 is no depression at all, how sad or depressed have you been today?"

Moreover, with the patient in the emergency room, one would want to know on a 0 to 10 scale, just how serious were the past suicide attempts, and how serious is this one? Using a similar scale, one can rapidly probe into how depressed, and how hopeless, the patient has been on prior attempts and how the patient is at this moment.

During an intake in the office, when patients claim to have a depression that they rate as –10, one needs to immediately inquire if the patient is suicidal. If the patients denies current active lethality, one can correct the patient by saying: "Perhaps we should rate you as a –9/10 or –9.5/10 today."

Dramatizing patients initially may rate their depression as –12, but they soon get the message that they need "to play the game

Figure 2.1

within the boundaries." When, infrequently, patients seem hesitant to apply numbers to a condition, one can say:

> Your guess would be better than mine, since you are the world's expert on you. I really value learning about your experience, and this will help me to understand your condition better so that I can treat you more effectively.

The visual analogue scale for depression is particularly helpful in assessing patients with so-called masked depression: patients with depression so profound as to drastically alter their activities of daily living and fuel their suicidal ideation, even though upon occasion they are able to flash a lovely Colgate smile and engage in socially sophisticated banter when a neighbor unexpectedly drops in, before going back to bed for another two weeks.

Patients are also very adept at rating on a 0 to –10 scale their prior episodes of depression. The patient's guess in such situations is going to be better than the clinician's. And patients very often have a clear picture of the severity of one episode of depression in comparison to another, even when separated by decades. Although one would like to have a 10-point scale rather than an 11-point scale, such researcher-friendly nuances are often lost on patients.

INFREQUENT ERRORS USING A VISUAL ANALOGUE SCALE AND OTHER SIMPLE PROBLEMS

Most patients very quickly do get it. However, some patients, perhaps inculcated into the Bo Derek tradition of 10 being the best and 0 being the worst, make scale reversal errors. But these reversals in practice are infrequent, and gentle prompting (especially when the clinical impression is at odds with the patient's proffered score) quickly corrects the improper use of the wrong end of the visual analogue scale. Some patients that are not quick learners need to be reminded each time that 10 is as much sadness or depression as anyone can bear.

For rapid-cycler or mixed-state bipolar patients that are depressed and manic at the same or different times, one can say: "On a scale of –10 being as depressed as one can be, 0 being no depression, and +10 being as manic as one can be, how would you rate yourself today?"

Patients can be both depressed and hypomanic at the same time, or these moods can alternate rapidly from one state to the next.

USING AN ANALOGUE SCALE FOR CONDITIONS OTHER THAN AFFECTIVE DISORDERS

For patients with co-morbid anxiety, it becomes quite easy to transpose the concept of self-rating in depression to a self-rating of anxiety, with +10 being as much anxiety as anyone can bear and 0 being no anxiety. When patients say both 6 and 7 in describing their mental state, one merely feeds back that you will use 6.5/10.

Patients with nicotine addiction or other substance use disorders can readily rate their urges to use, or cravings, as the cravings change with social setting and stress situations, again with 0 being no craving and +10 being an urge so strong that the use of some substance is almost inevitable.

One can also readily ask a patient to quantitate auditory halluci-nations, as a way of judging if he or she is receiving an adequate amount of antipsychotic medication:

On a scale of 0 to 10, with 10 being the very loudest your hallucinations can be, how loud are your hallucinations today? Do the voices seem to be further away now? Are you able to pay less attention to them? Are they any less frequent now since we have started the new medication?

USING PERCENTAGES TO RATE LETHALITY: EXPANDING THE UPPER END OF THE ANALOGUE SCALE

Clinicians working with suicidal outpatients may ask:

On a scale of 0% to 100%, where 100% means you are just about to commit suicide and 0% means you have no thoughts about suicide, how suicidal are you right now?

Experienced clinicians tend to hospitalize their patients when the likelihood of suicide is up to 95% or more. But obviously, each clinician needs to work out his or her own numbers system, and often each clinician needs to work out a system with each patient, too. Numbers don't seem to have an action-oriented meaning to patients, but obviously they can for clinicians. But there needs to be increased sensitivity to change at the upper (most dangerous end) of the scale. Here, in making an assessment, it's important to cut to the chase as quickly and as accurately as possible. Using a percentage scale is a very useful shortcut, especially when working within the confines of the 20-minute hour.

When lethality is an issue, the most important part of the scale is that at the top, between 9 and 10. Hence an expanded scale is helpful. The clinician using percentage has 101 theoretical data points, rather than 11, as in the 0 to 10 scale. Outpatients with strong suicidal ideation (and their clinicians) are acutely aware of the differences in their clinical state from 92% suicidal to 95% suicidal.

Patients sometimes can be truthful about "mere numbers" but not so forthcoming about asking for help (i.e., needing hospitalization). At times it is preferable to "let the numbers do the talking" (and decision making). Numbers can be an indirect but accurate way to gain access to the patient's feeling state.

Another example of the utility of an indirect clinical probe comes with a potentially help-repudiating patient that might not want to let on about how suicidal he or she has recently been. So one would ask the question: "Were you surprised that you survived?"

This is an excellent way of indirectly judging the implicit lethality of a recent attempt. Prior suicide attempts can also be parsed numerically, as an alternative to using terms like *gesture* or *failed attempt*, using a simple ratio of medical risk (high, moderate, to low rescuability; will inevitably be rescued, will probably be found, unlikely to be found while still alive), the risk/rescue ratio devised by Wiseman and Worden.

OTHER WAYS OF QUANTITATING CRUCIAL ASPECTS OF THE PATIENT'S ACTIVITIES OF DAILY LIVING

One can be informed quite quickly about the impact of a depressive episode on activities of daily living by asking the patient to quantitate certain aspects of daily living:

In the past month, how many days did you spend mostly in bed or on the couch? How many days did you not shower? Not floss your teeth? Not take all of your medicines? How many days were you crying for a considerable part of the day?

Without such quantification, the clinician doesn't really grasp the full dimension of the patient's dysfunction.

Chemical dependency patients can readily rate their consumption in bags of heroin per day or dollars spent; six packs or cases of beer per weekend, or bottles of Jack Daniels per week. And they can also quickly tell you about age of first use, heavy use, excessive use, and out-of-control use.

Quantitating delirium can be done by timing the number of seconds, and later minutes, a patient can stay engaged with the examiner before mentally drifting away. This is a brief, objective technique to use in observing a patient on a daily basis as a toxic encephalopathy clears. The longer (in seconds) that the patient can pay attention and stay increasingly focused, the more the clinician can rest assured that the delirium is clearing.

Although these quantitative examples do not all relate to *Diagnostic and Statistical Manual of Mental Disorders* (DSM-IV) criteria, they give a very personal touch to the way that, for example, depression can ravage an individual's life or delirium can cloud a patient's mind. Although there is yet no research "gold standard" to use to judge the face validity and unprompted repeat validity of the visual analogue scales for depression, or for the use of other semiquantitative questions for other clinical conditions, continued use readily validates both the utility and practicality of such tools as a quick way to better understand the world in which the patient is interacting and often suffering. Although a Beck or Montgomery-Asberg Depression Rating Scale (MADRS) is more authoritative than a visual analogue scale, sometimes "half a loaf is better than none."

MORE TRADITIONAL AND RAPID CLINICAL QUANTIFICATION MEASURES THAT ARE PARTICULARLY HELPFUL

There are a number of patient-rated clinical scales, often distributed to prescribers without charge by pharmaceutical companies, that can be very helpful in judging a patient's progress with, for example, his or her obsessive compulsive disorder. Three standardized and brief self-rating scales that are particularly helpful are the Yale Brown Obsessive Compulsive Scale (YBOC), which takes only a few minutes to rate change in obsessions and compulsions; the Adult Self-Report Scale (ASRS) Symptom Checklist for ADHD and ADD, a quick self-rating screening scale for attention deficit disorders; and finally, Hirschberg's Mood Disorder Questionnaire, a good screening instrument for a prior history of hypomanias. The patient's answers to 13 questions provide some helpful insight for patients with previously undiagnosed bipolar condition (Chapter 10). The mini-SPIN (Social Phobia INventory) is a three-item self-report with a cutoff of ≥ 6 that yields a sensitivity of 88% and a specificity of 90%.

The most frequently cited psychiatric rating scales, with an explanation about their use and time to administer and score, are available without charge on the web. Some pharmaceutical companies still offer a variety of paper-and-pencil rating scales to the clinician without charge.

SUMMARY

After the clinician spends a span of time with the patient he or she gradually develops a clinical picture of both the objective and subjective state of the patient, assuming that the right questions have been asked. But with the 20-minute hour in the new psychiatry, the clinician doesn't have the luxury of time.

Although there are multiple reasons to use numbers in medicine, the most compelling for the clinician in the 20-minute hour is the pressure of time. In the rapid pace of clinical practice, one needs to get access very rapidly to patients' perceptions of their interior state. Shortcuts to understanding are always useful in the hurried practice of clinical medicine.

Chapter 3

Setting the Contract

When money changes hands with some frequency, a contract is recommended. When there are expectations on both sides of the deal, and there are often high feelings involved, a contract is mandatory. Because most trainees and young professionals tend to see their patients in an institutional setting, there is often a tendency not to spend much time on the details of the contract. Certain details are routinely taken care of in a minimal manner by the clinic's administrative assistant in the context of informing the patient of his or her Health Insurance Portability and Accountability Act (HIPAA) rights. But the rights and responsibilities of being a patient in the clinic are rarely defined.

It is often a time-saver for the clinician to go over some aspects of the contract with the patient. This can be done in dribs and drabs throughout the first session, with punctuality the focus of one contract detail in the first session, and other matters in following sessions. Much about the contract is implicitly assumed by both parties, but assumptions can lead to lack of co-payments, not showing up on time, "did not keep appointments" (DNKAs) or same-day cancellations, and too frequent telephone calls about trivial matters. Trainees typically have many more of these problems from their patients than more seasoned clinicians, due to the seasoned clinician's willingness to make the implicit *explicit*.

One VA clinician with a part-time private practice establishes a contract with all of her patients by giving them a handout (courtesy of Luisa Skoble, MD, with modifications, in Table 3.1). Of note, the term *contract* is not used, but rather the practice information handout discloses activities outside of the practice session that could prove to be problematic.

Table 3.1 Handout Concerning Practice Information

These are policies I have set up to manage my practice. This information will
help clarify the mutual responsibilities in the therapeutic relationship you
are about to enter into.

Insurance authorization and financial obligations: It is important
that you verify your mental health benefits with your insurance provider.
Most insurance plans now require you to get prior authorization for a
mental health visit. It is your responsibility to obtain this authorization.
Services rendered here without proper authorization will be billed to you
in full, and you will be responsible for all of those unauthorized costs.

Telephone messages are recorded with the time/date and stored in a
confidential place. Voice mail is checked once or more each afternoon.
Please leave times when you will be available to receive calls and provide
the appropriate telephone number(s). I will make every effort to return
your call within one business day. For telephone calls lasting longer than
five minutes, you will be billed on a pro-rated professional hourly basis.
I do not do e-mail with my patients.

Urgent matters can be handled through the hospital page operator,
who knows how to reach me. I do not communicate with my patients by
telephone for anything but the most exceptional issues, such as a frightening
drug reaction or uncontrollable increase in pressure to make a suicide
attempt. I do not switch my patients from one medication to another over
the telephone. Almost all of our work together will be handled through an
office visit.

Emergencies occasionally may happen. I am not in full-time practice, so I am
not set up to handle inpatient care or walk-in appointments. If your call is
about an emergency situation and I am unable to return your call quickly
enough, please report to an emergency room for immediate attention.

Refill requests left on my voice mail system should include the medication
name(s), strength(s), and directions on the label of the prescription bottle(s),
date last filled, and your birth date along with the pharmacy telephone
number, including area code if it is in a different part of the state. I do
reserve the right to refuse to renew prescriptions if you do not have a
scheduled appointment already set up.

Being on time is really important, because if you are tardy there may not
be enough time to adequately evaluate you and treat you appropriately in a
shortened appointment. Because other patients also have time pressures,
I cannot let you use up some of another patient's time. Occasionally a
clinical emergency may cause me to be late for my patients, but this should
be a very rare event.

Missed appointments: If you need to change or cancel an appointment,
it must be done with at least 24 hours lead time, so that your time slot can
be filled by someone else. Regardless of the reason, you will be charged and
expected to pay in full for the missed session, as insurance companies do
not reimburse for missed sessions.

Table 3.1 (continued) Handout Concerning Practice Information

Paperwork, such as disability forms and notes to the employer, will be handled in the beginning of this or the very next session as time allows. There will be a pro-rated professional hourly fee for those reports that cannot be handled within a session, as reports not done face-to-face in a session are not covered by insurance.

Payment is always due in full before each session, with no exceptions. For most patients, this is merely a co-pay. Unfortunately, this is not a sliding-scale practice and credit is not extended. In most instances, your insurance company will be billed directly for services rendered. With certain companies, however, you might have to submit the bill yourself, in which case your monthly statement will include all the necessary information required for your reimbursement.

Termination of treatment can occur by:

1. Mutual agreement that treatment is no longer indicated or beneficial
2. Missing two or more appointments without letting me know at least 24 hours in advance about your need to cancel. Canceling on the very day of an appointment counts as a missed appointment.
3. Behaving in a way that is not appropriate to this kind of practice. Other grounds for termination may arise.

I acknowledge that I have read, understand, and accept the above policies. I authorize the release of relevant medical information to my insurance provider to facilitate claim processing and claim reimbursement. I agree that, regardless of insurance status, I am ultimately responsible for the balance on my account for any professional services rendered.

_____   _____
Signature   Date

CONTRACT ADD-ONS

In addition to the more formal handout, the clinician can make amendments to the contract as it serves the need of patient care.

For the patient making *suicide* gestures, the clinician may wish to tell the patient:

> Mrs. A, you have made another suicide gesture. I know this has a number of meanings for you and served as a means of communication. But to me, it means that our psychotherapy may not be working out very well. So if this happens again, I reserve the right to refer you to another therapist.

Years later, a number of patients have told me that this part of the contract allowed them to pull up short and not follow through with another suicide gesture, because they did not want to terminate the therapeutic relationship.

For the patient with a *serious alcohol problem*, the clinician may be tempted to be supportive with the well-intentioned hope that when the patient is out of crisis, he or she will stop drinking or using some substances. Having tried this for years, I can assure you that this is merely co-dependent behavior, in which the clinician is facilitating the patient's delaying getting into successful treatment. With alcoholic patients, or other substance abusers, the clinician may want to say:

> Mr. B, we have worked together for quite a time now, and I have tried to be quite supportive as you have openly shared with me your struggle to become sober. But it should be clear to both of us now that you are not winning the battle, and I am not being helpful enough just with our outpatient psychotherapy in solving this giant problem. I want to be able to continue to work with you, but you need to get treatment specific for your substance use first.
>
> So let's set up a deadline by which you will get into substance use treatment, and if you don't, I'll have to terminate our treatment. In the meantime, here are the names and the telephone numbers of the places for you to call. Let's hope that your next session won't be our last one working together.

So far, all the conditions considered (suicide gestures, getting drunk, being late, not paying the co-pay, calling often for matters that should be dealt with in the office, berating the office staff on the telephone and shouting at them in the office, being a repeat DNKA) have all focused on violations of the contract, either the original practice information handout or the *ad hoc* contractual add-on. But should there be a contract about how a patient behaves in the office?

CONTRACTS ABOUT MATERIAL TO BE DISCUSSED IN THE SESSION

In the heyday of psychoanalysis, the contract itself was widely discussed in books and presentations. There was a consensus that the psychotherapy contract should be explicitly extended to matters such as sharing all dreams with the analyst, not making any voluntary changes in employment while in treatment, talking openly about feelings and fantasies about the analyst, not withholding or editing thoughts and feelings about other important events or life phases, and not talking about one's analysis in any detail with one's friends. Some contracts prohibited the patient from marrying while still in treatment!

Now, the consensus is that contracts for what material the patient should bring up in the session, and how to navigate life's milestones need not be rigidly defined for the patient. This is particularly the case for short-term work and medication management.

If the patient comes late to an appointment, not too much time, if any, should be spent on the reason for tardiness, as this distracts from the remaining time needed for assessment and medication management. It is important to tell the patient, should you feel there is not enough time for the usual components of the session, that you would like to do more, but that the patient has not allowed sufficient time.

Nonpayment issues need to be addressed early on, and if need be, often. Nonpayment has multiple dynamic meanings, including expressing anger at the therapist, punishing him or her for the perceived ineffectiveness of treatment. Nonpayment can also be the expression of the narcissistic wish that the patient deserves to be paid, not the therapist, since it is the patient that is the special one. Discussing the nonpayment may help the patient to understand the behavior, and will help the therapist to decide whether or not to terminate treatment.

Material within the 20-minute hour needs to focus, first and foremost, on the patient's signs and symptoms, semiquantitative measures of improving or being stuck on a plateau. It is the responsibility of both the patient and the clinician to be certain that, together, they have been able to understand what is most important in the patient's environment.

Some patients can, on their own initiative, paint a vivid picture of their activities, feelings, and progress (or lack of it) on their path toward wholeness/wellness. Other patients need to have the material pulled out of them. Whatever, it is the clinician's responsibility to become aware of relevant aspects of the patient's interior life, feelings, and significant relationships. Indeed, by the end of each session the clinician must have elicited material on the biopsychosocial dimensions of the patient's world to better understand the patient's plight.

In summary, the contract now is more about a business relationship than about issues relating to understanding dynamics. The contract is a very useful tool that assists in maintaining a climate conducive to a therapeutic working relationship. The patient should have an explicit contract dealing with his or her responsibilities. The clinician has an implicit contract: to understand and help the patient cope with the problems and chief complaints that the patient brought to the session when seeking help.

Chapter 4

Decisions, Decisions

Clinical care is about making major decisions, for and with the patient, often based on fragmentary information using intuition, buttressed by experience. While this is true for all branches of medicine, it is particularly true for psychological medicine. This chapter explores the options the clinician must choose among in the rapid evaluation of an outpatient, starting with the initial encounter with the patient, and ending with the decision to accept the patient for treatment. It is hoped that a systematic listing of these decisions will allow for more efficient use of the limited time available to perform the initial evaluation. The clinician must remember that an evaluation means an encounter to see if the patient is suitable for that clinician to treat. If not, recommendations must be made for referral elsewhere.

DOES THE PATIENT REPRESENT A SAFETY ISSUE?

The patient has been sent to the clinician's office to get help for the problem, but is the office the right place for the patient to be seen? When encountering an outpatient for the first time, the initial set of decisions, often dealt with in nanoseconds, concern safety. Is this patient suitable for evaluation in an office setting or is an ER better? Is it all right for the patient to sit by himself or herself alone in the office? Will the clinician be safe to sit unaccompanied in the examining room with the patient? Is the patient suicidal? Is he or she armed? Floridly psychotic? Intoxicated?

In most cases, the initial encounter is not fraught with such volatile matters.

But all mental health workers have been assiduously drilled in the axiom based on Maslow's hierarchy of needs: safety first, security next, and fulfillment later on. Since this book is a primer, it will not focus much attention on this otherwise important issue of emergency management of the patient out of control, since such training and relevant information are available elsewhere.

IS THERE READILY AVAILABLE COROLLARY INFORMATION?

The next set of decisions focus on the practical issue of other sets of information about the patient. Is the patient well known to the clinic or some of the personnel working in the office? Is there an old chart somewhere (for example, if the patient's clinical record has a low serial number)? Is it worth the time to summon the old chart and review it?

If the patient is sitting in the waiting room with someone who might be a significant other, should that person be invited into the examining room along with the patient? The patient can usually make that decision on the spot, but it is probably a mistake not to address this matter when meeting the patient for the first time. The availability of an old chart summary or an articulate significant other can often be a time-saver, leading to more informed questions to ask the patient, and more informed active listening, too.

Some patients can give a comprehensive overview of their symptoms as they have evolved over time, the various psychoactive medications they have taken, in what amount, and with what side effects and main effect. Other patients may be relatively poor informants. They may be too depressed, unmotivated, and hopeless, or too irritable or openly psychotic to be fully involved in the diagnostic process. Here the decision to seek correlative information from family seems easy.

For the inarticulate patient, if he or she has a significant other still present in the waiting room, will it be worth the extra time to ask that person some questions (with the patient's concordance), or will this just be an opportunity for the significant other to ventilate and otherwise take up precious time?

IS COMPREHENSIVE INFORMATION
REALLY NEEDED?

Even with the most cooperative patient, there still may be additional information necessary to really understand the patient's illness. Fortunately, most routine evaluation protocols make this next decision easy: Even though there may be nothing in the history to trigger probing into certain areas, still most intake protocols require inquiry into issues such as substance abuse, physical/sexual abuse, and suicidality. And surprisingly, some patients are able to mask their depression and lethality, so asking about suicidal ideation is always wise on the initial evaluation. Moreover, if the patient is suicidal, it is always wise to inquire about homicidal ideation.

Another decision that is often postponed or neglected, if there are no ready clues to relevance in the intake history, is a simple search for a biological basis for the patient's mental disorder, including hypothyroidism, syphilis, lupus cerebritis, AIDS, or some other low-frequency condition. Is it worth the extra time to explain the blood tests and write out the laboratory request slip?

HOW BEST TO RELATE TO THE PATIENT

After the patient has settled down, with or without the significant other from the waiting room, and the interview is beginning, one has to discuss what name the patient wishes to be called by. The next set of decisions concerns how best to relate to the patient. The earliest initial contact with the patient often sets the tone of the working relationship. Is it worthwhile to change one's usual style of relating to patients for the sake of increased rapport with a specific patient?

This primer on how to make the most of the 20-minute hour assumes that the reader is knowledgeable about the basics of the interviewing process. The point that we address here is that the style the interviewer uses, if correctly selected, can greatly increase both the amount of information retrieved in a timely manner and the rapid development of positive transference, usually quite helpful in medication maintenance.

With adolescents, one needs to be more informal than with a young adult. With the hard of hearing, cognitively impaired, intellectually challenged, openly paranoid, or extremely flirtatious, one needs to make a rapid adjustment in interviewing style to best fit the needs of the clinical situation.

With an uninvolved patient, because of ambivalence in being in the clinician's office, or because he or she has been forced to attend the session, information retrieval can be quite inefficient. One must make the decision on whether or not to quietly confront the issue head on. Often taking time to rapidly deal with such an underlying issue can end up saving time.

IS THE PATIENT SUITABLE FOR TREATMENT IN YOUR CLINICAL SETTING?

Meeting the patient's expectations and needs is often a complex matter.

As one completes the initial evaluation, one must decide which type of setting is most suitable for the patient. For example, most, but not all, patients with schizophrenia are best managed in a community mental health-type setting. Such a facility can provide not only medication management, but also ancillary psychotherapy, case management, ready access to clozapine treatment if required, occupational counseling, sheltered workshops, easier access to Section 8 housing and food stamps, and assistance with Social Security Disability Income (SSDI) applications and reduced cost public transportation. Certain patients with bipolar disorder and borderline personality disorders will also do better in a community mental health-like setting.

Patients with a past history of frequent noncompliance with appointments (often with a persistently chaotic lifestyle) may also not be appropriate for a solo private practice because of their need for frequent unscheduled visits or same-day/next-day appointments. Psychiatric emergency rooms, certain community mental health centers with crisis intervention services, and some primary care physician offices may be better set up to accommodate such patients.

Other patients that want one-stop integrated biomedical and psychological care may do better in a private practice setting, even one that does not directly accept health care insurance payment. Such patients pay out of pocket for their weekly 45-minute sessions since they have access to discretionary income. But many well-to-do patients chafe at managed care restrictions on their visits but still are not willing to pass up using their health insurance "entitlement."

The decision about appropriateness of fit can be a difficult one for the clinician.

WHAT TO DO WHEN THE PATIENT IS 14, OR 16, MINUTES LATE FOR THE SESSION

Should the patient be squeezed into the schedule, if all subsequent patients that day will end up being seen later than at their expected time? Time, at least for the clinician, is a finite element and can't be expanded. How late is late? Can an adequate initial evaluation or follow-up visit be done in a very limited time? If the clinician sees the patient in a foreshortened session and misses an otherwise remarkable finding, he or she is still responsible for the visit, even if the patient was responsible for being late. Most clinics have clear guidelines on whether or not to let the patient see the clinician and whether or not to charge for "too late to see the clinician," "no-shows," and "late cancels." It is often up to the clinician to make the decision on whether a late patient should be seen at all that day if there is inadequate time to perform the usual visit. Scheduling 15-minute breaks scattered throughout the day allows for more flexibility for patient care catch-ups.

WHICH MEDICATION TO CHOOSE

After the initial rapport has been established, the necessary information to formulate a diagnosis collected, and a contract for a treatment plan negotiated, the choice of which psychopharmacological agent, if appropriate, must be made. Should the patient have depression as a primary illness, for example, there are six selective serotonin reuptake inhibitors, four serotonin-norepinephrine reuptake inhibitors, nine different tricyclic antidepressants, and four other antidepressants (bupropion, maprotoline, mirtazepine, and trazodone). Although familiarity with one or two antidepressant agents may be a good reason for making the choice for the primary care physician, the specialist prescriber needs to have more options. Here the choice needs to focus on the patient's economic needs (hefty co-pays or lack of an insurance drug benefit may make the initial or refill prescriptions unaffordable). The current year's formularies of the large managed behavioral health care companies are generally readily available. They place psychopharmacological agents into three tiers, from least to most expensive by co-pays.

Another determinant of which drug to choose relates to the patient's comorbid medical condition(s). Obviously, one would avoid a tricyclic antidepressant in a patient with second-degree heart block or a recent myocardial infarction; or a monoamine oxidase inhibitor in a vegetarian with a restricted diet dependent on cheese for protein. One might make the decision to avoid a selective serotonin reuptake inhibitor (SSRI) in a patient with decreased libido on a prior failed SSRI drug trial, interrupted because of sexual side effects. One might avoid nefazodone in a patient with liver disease or dysfunction; or venlafaxine in a patient with pseudo-tumor cerebri (because of possible elevation of blood pressure); and so forth.

Still another factor in the decision about which antidepressant to choose is the issue of patient preference. Some patients can deliver a sophisticated pharmacogenetic family history on what did and did not work on their identical twin, maternal grandmother, or aunt. When this information is initially available, it does help to inform decision making. All too often, such information is only available by the time the first antidepressant has failed.

Patients often have strong predetermined preferences based on their response to the billions of dollars the pharmaceutical industry spends annually on direct-to-consumer advertising. Also, some patients develop strong preferences based on remissions achieved by neighbors or business cohorts. Dissuading such an "informed" patient may take away time better spent on other aspects of the treatment plan.

HOW FREQUENTLY TO SCHEDULE THE RETURN VISIT

Before the onset of managed behavioral health care, scheduling of a return visit for a patient with depression was relatively simple: again this week, next week, or the week after next. Now with limitations posed by certain MCOs, there may be assiduous paperwork required after the sixth visit or even the first visit. Many clinicians tell the patient that this particular session may need to focus mainly on filling out insurance forms (or for SSDI eligibility, temporary disability insurance, special housing request, etc.). These cumbersome "Request for Subsequent Care" forms were set up by MCOs as a barrier to utilization to decrease their mental health costs, and they have been effective.

But given the lack of forms or telephone calls to prove medical necessity of the visit, ideally when should the patient be scheduled for a return visit? How does one make such a determination? The American Psychiatric Association guidelines suggest the patient initially be seen at least three times in three months by a clinician (type unspecified).

Obviously patient need and patient preference always play a major role in determining when the patient should next be seen. But in making this decision, the clinician needs to know that there are many different models to choose from in determining when to follow up on medication management. For example, some busy community mental health clinics handling acute episodes for patients with mainly affective or anxiety disorders tend to see a return visit patient started on an SSRI after six weeks unless there are unacceptable side effects. In the meantime, the patient may have been seen by a therapist. After six weeks on medication, either it will be effective in the dose prescribed, or it will be in a subsequent six weeks with a higher dosage. Alternatively, if the patient has had pesky side effects after the initial six weeks, then the medication can be changed to one of a different class. At the third visit, three months after the initial visit, if the patient has not achieved remission, then one could switch to a different class of medication, increase the dosage again, or augment.

This clearly is a "health of the public" approach rather than a "boutique" approach with its weekly visits, but the community mental health center (CMHC) model does have the benefit of dramatically increasing access to psychiatric care. If visits are spaced out, then more patients can be served and guideline-congruent care can be rendered, with space available for emergency/urgent visits that occasionally develop. When the patient is considerably improved but not yet in remission, then a two-month return may suffice, while for patients stable in their course (perhaps only partially improved with a refractory depression), visits at three-month intervals may suffice.

Dealing with patients intolerant to many medications, or refractory to even high dosages of medication, presents a real challenge for medication management, but such patients' chronicity usually does not impact on patient flow or time needed to see the patient. Indeed, patients who become quite familiar because of their lack of response to numerous medication trials are often much easier to fit into the 20-minute hour than new patients seen for their initial visits.

Other clinicians will prefer to see all their new patients at least every two weeks until well, rather than using the CMHC model. In such settings, often the biweekly patient, impatient with slow improvement, may push the clinician to switch medications before an adequate therapeutic trial has been accomplished. These are important decisions of style for the psychiatrist to make, with no outcome studies available for firm guidance.

HOW THOROUGH DOES DOCUMENTATION OF INFORMED CONSENT NEED TO BE?

After the decision about which medication to use and the interval till the next visit, a chart note needs to be completed. Even though there is time pressure to move on to the next patient, it is still important for the legal protection of the prescriber to indicate in the chart that the patient understands that there are risks of adverse events from the prescribed medication. The prescriber needs to choose whether to use the standard "I have discussed the adverse effects of medication X with the patient and he/she understands the risks and benefits involved" or an alternative, such as "I have discussed the risks to the patient of medication X, and I feel he/she is making an informed decision."

One may also wish to add to either of the above, for example:

> The patient understands that Lamictal can cause an extremely severe skin rash; that lithium can cause weight gain, thyroid problems, and kidney problems, all three conditions to be closely monitored; that Ambien can cause transient psychotic reaction; and that Risperidone can cause tardive dyskinesia, involving twitching for the face or extremities, etc.

There are no uniformly accepted standards for the prescriber to follow, but it would be a mistake not to use some type of routine informed consent statement in the chart.

HOW TO MONITOR PATIENTS FOR VARIOUS IATROGENIC MEDICAL COMPLICATIONS

The most recently described adverse event prescribers have had to learn to grapple with is the metabolic syndrome. There have been multiple national conferences to develop guidelines for patients started on second-generation antipsychotic agents because of their potential for triggering or inducing diabetic ketoacidosis, hyperlipidemia, and weight gain. Some guidelines call for measuring the patient's girth (problems if more than 35 inches for women and 40 inches for men), the hemoglobin Hgb A1c, various lipid levels, the patient's body mass index (BMI), and the patient's weight at baseline and thence monthly (to make certain the patient is not gaining more than a pound a week, with six pounds being the cutoff for a decision to change medications). With so many guidelines floating around, the prescriber must choose which ones to regularly employ in his or her practice.

There are also informally established, or institutionally established, guidelines for monitoring for lithium (Li++ levels, thyroid stimulation hormone [TSH], blood urea nitrogen [BUN], creatinine, and weight); carbamazepine (tegretol levels, complete blood count [CBC] and platelets, and liver function tests); Trileptal (Na+); Depakote (valproic acid, CBC, liver function tests [LFTs], and weight); and nefazodone (LFTs). Although there are usually agreed upon guidelines for the first 6 to 12 months, the prescriber needs to decide on how carefully to monitor these parameters.

These are just some of the murky areas of decision making that impact on the patient's brief office visit, or on the effectiveness of use of time in the brief office visit. There often are no firm guidelines for the clinician to invoke, but wrestling with the problem beforehand can improve efficient use of time and "office flow."

Chapter 5

Psychoeducation/Teaching

The New Psychiatry has taken a 180-degree shift in emphasis, compared to psychiatric practice in the era of the 50-minute hour. It used to be that insight was the main focus of a psychiatrist's work, along with medication if indicated. The clinician would lend his or her observing ego, and guide the patient in painstaking introspection. The question "How does that make you feel?" was used a lot. There was no sense of urgency (unless, of course, the patient was psychotic, suicidal, or gravely disabled). During the 50-minute hour, the clinician was relatively passive, and the patient had the responsibility of learning. "Spoon-feeding" the patient with information was derided.

Now, in the era of the 20-minute hour, there is much more urgency to get the work done, with limited length of sessions, and limited number of sessions. The learning process needs to be fast forwarded to MAX. There is a growing consensus that psychoeducation is essential to maximize treatment impact, with considerable literature on psychoeducation for patients with schizophrenia and bipolar disorder, as well as with other chronic medical and psychiatric conditions. Psychoeducation is recognized as part of an evidence-based treatment package.

For example, the Texas Algorithm Program includes educational programs to teach the patient, and if possible the family, about the nature of the disorder, how to recognize signs of relapse, how best to manage it, and treatment options.

In the multicenter STEP-BD trial run by Gary Sachs, MD, for 4,361 bipolar patients, at the onset of clinical treatment, all patients are taught about their disorder. Each receives an educational video, a self-reporting procedure, and a written treatment plan. Patients with bipolar disorder, for example, can be taught how to identify early symptoms of relapse, and the importance of seeking prompt treatment when this occurs. Part of the educational emphasis is understanding the patient's health belief model (which sometimes may be quite bizarre) and sharing more conventional health belief models.

PSYCHOEDUCATIONAL GOALS

First-line goals of psychoeducation include illness awareness, recognition of patient-specific prodromal symptoms, the importance of treatment adherence, the utility of relapse prevention, and the importance of preventing suicide. Second-line goals are stress management, avoidance of alcohol and street drugs, and promoting lifestyle regularity, for example, social rhythm therapy. Third-line goals are maintaining progress, coping with psychosocial stressors, dealing with past consequences of episodes, coping with residual subsyndromal symptoms and impairment, and finally, increasing well-being and quality of life.

Such training is similar to the disease management one might anticipate for a patient with diabetes. There is an effort "to make the playing field more level," to use a collaborative care model, with patients trained to come to each session with a filled-out self-rating form, so the clinician can do an evaluation in about four minutes. This allows more time for talking with patients, for the development and maintenance of rapport, rather than just interrogating the patient about a panoply of symptoms.

Thus, clinician and patient are working in a partnership to help improve the patient's outcome. Now psychiatrists and other clinicians sometimes are hoarse at the end of the day from giving mini-lectures and otherwise being very active in the session in the educational process. Sensitivity to the patient's plight and understanding the patient's dynamics, however, are still as important as ever.

Although the patient's gaining insight is still very much valued, the gold standard has become *measurable change in behavior*. In the past, too many patients gained lots of insight into their behavior, but didn't change it or clinically improve. Now managed care organizations (MCOs) require evaluation of behavioral change as part of their ongoing determination of medical necessity. And the Joint Commission on Accreditation of Health Care Organizations (JCAHO) mandates that goals and observable behavioral changes be charted on all psychiatric inpatients.

In a practice of medication management mixed with some psychotherapy, teaching is no longer just by the Socratic method. Instructions on what to do, where to look for information, what books to read, and what Web sites to focus on now have a real place in the clinician's armamentarium.

THE STANCE OF MCOS IN PSYCHOEDUCATION

MCOs and their shareholders have no committed interest in supporting the training of residents and the education of medical students or others. They are invested in setting standards about what they are willing to pay for. The MCOs, moreover, have realized that patients need to acquire a cognitive map of their disease and its treatment, that is, an understanding of the role of medication and the benefits to outcome of continuity of care.

What is the impetus for having patients learn about their disorders? Patients that participate in disease management cost the MCOs less. This is particularly true for those with chronic illnesses, including psychiatric disorders. Informed patients are associated with improvement on a variety of measures of quality of life. They stay healthier longer, utilize fewer doctor's visits, and have lower overall medical costs. Many patients with years of "veteran status" with their illness can be knowledgeable, but patients newly diagnosed with bipolar or panic disorder, for example, have much to learn, as their diagnosis comes as a shock. Some patients with a long-standing refractory depression have never even heard the term *treatment-resistant depression*. Nor do many rapid cyclers or ultra-rapid cyclers know terminology important to understanding their illness. Many patients with affective illness do not understand the pernicious impact that substance use plays in the perpetuation of their illness, and need to learn about that. Treatment is simpler to implement when patients become better-informed consumers of psychiatric care.

Along with psychotherapy, consultation, medication management, and hypnosis, psychoeducation is one of the activities that clinicians have at their disposal. *Psychoeducation* is a new term, and as such it is a relatively new activity for many clinicians. Patients need to be informed about the nature of their disorder, what support groups could be helpful, and where and when they meet. Prescribers also need to teach about the benefits and risks of medication.

Documentation about the teaching of adverse effects of medication is essentially required, to prove that the teaching has taken place. "If it isn't documented," MCOs and plaintiffs' attorneys state, "it didn't happen." To document their teaching about possible adverse operative and perioperative outcomes, some cardiac surgeons now routinely videotape their informed consents, since their patients typically remember only about 25% of what they were told to expect.

Given the infrequent visits that are allowed for psychiatric patients (which often means a considerable number of weeks between sessions), how can one continue to keep the patient involved in the therapeutic process? Homework of various sorts includes journals to keep, daily mood charts to fill out, books to read, workbooks to follow, support groups to go to, and Web sites to visit. All these assignments keep patients involved in the therapeutic process, helping them to remember to keep the next appointment and, as appropriate, take their medicines.

MCOs do not pay for fulfillment-type therapy, such as marital counseling or Big Sur marathon encounter groups. But MCOs do pay for issues related to safety and security. So psychoeducation skirts the fulfillment issue, because it's not traditional psychotherapy but it does enhance outcomes.

FINDING THE PATIENT'S LEVEL

Many clinicians, lamentably, either talk with the patient in too simplistic a fashion or, more likely, talk over the patient's head. Less educated and especially less intelligent patients generally want explanations about what their problem is and what the medicine does, simplified to the level of symptoms and their relief. More intellectually sophisticated patients often want the aforementioned plus explanations at the molecular level. Their interest may be in both their own improvement and the relevant neuroscience.

Just as a teacher uses different techniques at the bedside or in the amphitheatre, he or she uses different vocabulary and approaches for medical students as compared to fellows, so clinicians must quickly be able to adjust their interactions to meet the cognitive and developmental level of the patient. Knowing the patient's level of education and his or her most recent or favorite gainful employment role helps the clinician to make a rapid adjustment targeted to the patient's level of listening, understanding, and relating. Since time is of the essence, learning rapidly, from the patient and with the patient, is essential.

Unfortunately, there is rarely enough time for extended psychoeducation. Hence the role of "bibliotherapy," referring the patient to carefully chosen textbooks, patient-oriented books, series of articles, or vetted Web sites. Many times it is appropriate to say to the patient: "Your mission, should you accept it, is to spend 10 hours reading about your bipolar condition before our next visit. Here is my basic Web site that has a great deal of interesting material on it."

TEACHING AIDS

As will be spelled out in Chapter 6 on shortcuts, prepared teaching aids are absolutely necessary to help propel the patient toward a desired outcome. Web sites, books, handouts, and peer group meetings from first-line patient-sponsored organizations should all be part of the psychiatrist's repertory. Letting patients rove about searching for reliable resources sometimes slows down the healing process, and in a world of limited clinician-patient contacts, a lack of active teaching may sometimes be responsible for a less favorable outcome.

Self-help groups have refined their educational programs to meet the needs of the consumer. The National Alliance for the Mentally Ill, the National Depressive and Manic Depressive Association, the Anxiety Disorders Association of America, the National Mental Health Association, the Obsessive Compulsive Foundation, and the Trichotillomania Society, among others, have superb pamphlets as well as well-prepared annual meetings that are up to date with the best science, explained in patient-friendly terms.

Many such groups usually have strong scientific advisory boards involving some of the nation's preeminent scientists; the best such organizations also provide their members with periodic newsletters that are lively, informative, and quite up to date. These organizations are very inexpensive for patients to join, and many have local support and education groups that meet on a regular basis in convenient locations that are free of professional sponsorship.

Some Veterans Affairs (VA) Mental Hygiene Clinics have a Family Education Day each year that focus on teaching family members about various aspects of common major psychiatric disorders and current treatment regimens, which shortcuts problems and assists in favorable outcomes.

DOCERE MEANS "TO TEACH"

The term *doctor* comes from the Latin word *docere*, which means "to teach." Patients who have good teachers as their physicians are more likely to have better outcomes. Clinicians have long been accustomed to their role as teachers—supervising residents or trainees and giving curbstone consults to their younger colleagues. They are also accustomed to helping their patients learn about themselves, their dynamics, their plight in perspective, and their role in perpetuating their illness, if applicable.

Grade school teachers and college professors have their lesson plans for the day, which can be somewhat altered by discussion that comes from the class. So clinicians need to have their goals for material to be covered by the challenged learner as well as the much more sophisticated patient, with the idea that all lesson plans should help increase adherence to the patient's therapeutic plan.

Clinicians in academia, suddenly finding themselves in full-time private practice, often do not miss the formal teaching role, because sessions with patients often have a didactic component. And as it is true in the classroom where teachers both teach and learn from their students, so it is in sessions with patients, always in a learning environment.

Teaching or psychoeducation is only valuable if it improves rapport, allows the therapeutic medication trial to become part of a collaborative effort, helps control dysfunctional affect, improves goal-oriented behavior, or makes a favorable outcome as a mutual goal. Thus, information not targeted to such a program may well be on overload. When time is short, one needs to keep on target. Getting open, honest, and rapid feedback becomes crucial.

HOW OFTEN DO THE LESSONS NEED TO BE REPEATED?

One might think, since patients usually seem to be paying rapt attention in their session, that telling the patient once about taking the medication only as prescribed will suffice. However, inpatient studies indicate that drug compliance in some instances may be less than 40%. Outpatient adherence studies also indicate an appallingly low rate of adherence. One is prompted to say, "OK, but my patients do take their medications as prescribed." Beware, this is often not the case.

Patients frequently have very strong sociocultural biases against "taking too much medication." For example, trusted family members may tell a very sick patient that he or she is being overmedicated (even though he or she still is very symptomatic). Or they will tell the patient who is finally in remission that now is the time to stop taking the medication since the patient is well. Between seemingly caring but misinformed families and antimedication cultural biases, there are many factors that keep some patients undermedicated, at times to the surprise of their prescriber. Similarly, there are also many forces that drive patients toward overmedication. In a busy practice, there is often at least one of each type of patient per day.

How much teaching does it take to have a patient become medication adherent? Obviously, the answer depends on the patient, his or her psychodynamics and culture, plus familial biases. Drug companies are always trying to change the habits and practice patterns of physicians, obviously a highly educated group. These corporations annually spend billions of dollars to try to convince prescribers of the value of their medication *de jour*. Product detailers often figure they need 26 contacts of varying types to begin to change prescribing habits. The message: It often takes a surprisingly large number of contacts with a patient to get him or her to understand and value the role that properly prescribed medication plays in recovery.

Thus, in the short 20-minute hour there needs to be some time in many or most sessions for psychoeducation. One needs to reiterate the treatment plan and goals, inquire about adherence issues, and set up a new lesson plan as needed.

CONCLUSION

Psychoeducation is an important part of quality medication management. Some part of the initial and follow-up visits should be devoted to this activity. Psychoeducation also provides the patient with a cognitive map of the illness process, allowing for the development of some sense of mastery in *terra incognita*.

Chapter 6

Shortcuts

There is no shortcut to having a special relationship with a patient. Accurate empathy, nonpossessive warmth, real concern, and positive interest and regard are common characteristics of all good clinicians, regardless of their theoretical orientation or staff position. There is no faking it. Whether spending 2 minutes with the patient or 50, the way the clinician relates to the patient from the very beginning of the relationship sets the tone for all that follows.

The information and advice here are merely aids to give the busy clinician more quality time to appreciate the person who is a patient. All patients have, by definition, a disorder, as described in a textbook. But the patient's illness is unique, and reflects how he or she is coping with that disease. Understanding the patient and the illness is the art of medicine. If one is feeling frantic, one's empathy and intuition are not fully engaged.

Every clinician struggles with time management issues. Even in a 50-minute hour, with articulate, motivated, and needy patients, there are instances when there is just not enough time. But with the 50-minute hour, there is a built-in 10-minute cushion before the next patient, so running a few minutes over usually poses no problem. But if one is seeing two to four patients in an hour, that cushion has virtually evaporated.

As any host at a party knows, some guests take a long time to warm up, while others are bubbly right away. Some guests take forever with their good-byes, while others exit cleanly and quickly. So it is with patients. Some need the clinician to jump-start the session, others almost start the session, even with emotionally loaded material, out in the hallway. And at session's end, some patients' closing of session comments can occupy a seemingly endless two to three minutes or more. Since the clinician's time is precious, there are a few techniques, quickly learned, that are effective, efficient, and consumer-friendly.

This chapter focuses on ways of getting more content into a session and ending it promptly. Time can't be squeezed or compressed, so the clinician has to find ways to be maximally efficient in the allotted time frame in order to keep the office both on schedule and peaceful: a pleasant place for healer and the seeker of healing to optimize their time together.

USING THE HALLWAY TO GET THE SHOW ROLLING (WHILE MAINTAINING CONFIDENTIALITY)

Some clinician offices are located very close to the reception area, but some others are a two-minute walk down the hall, yet both are allotted the same amount of time from one patient to the next. What should the clinician do? How should he or she even out the playing field?

Obviously, there are limits within the confines of confidentiality and social manners. However, it is possible to "get the ball rolling" by bring up a subject that is noncontroversial, as a way of jump-starting the process. One should try to avoid emotional "hot button" topics in the hallway. But especially after the clinician knows the patient, it may be useful to ask about important but neutral subjects in a natural conversational manner while walking briskly to the office.

BEING A CONVERSATIONALIST AND HOW TO END ON TIME

One of the most trying of all the tasks facing the clinician is how to minimize endless social chatter at the end of the session or how to postpone an interesting topic that the patient has raised just after the end of the allocated time. This is particularly difficult with the obsessive patient who often only picks up on his or her own cues, and not those of others; and with the needy dependent patient that seems to live more in the session than outside of it.

Clinicians have usually had years of professional training in interviewing techniques. But before that, they have had two to three decades of social skills training in conversation at home and school. Thus, these early and long-term experiences have imprinted rules such as:

1. You should never interrupt the other person.
2. You should not dismiss another's earnest or juicy new conversational gambit (even if it prolongs the dialogue).
3. The termination of a conversation should be by mutual consent.
4. You should never tell someone who is talking that his or her time is up.

It is difficult to put aside such proscriptions, but in the interest of time management and keeping to the 20-minute hour, these archaic social conventions have to be set aside. It is important, of course, that one maintains social decorum. So, a brief apology is always offered, such as: "I'm sorry, but time is up for today. Let's talk more about this and other questions that come up next time!"

If the patient still lingers after giving of the prescription for medication as the ceremony of the closure of the session, one can then say: "I look forward to seeing you next time, but now I must finish my writing up of our session."

A final alternative is: "Please close the door as you go out so I can concentrate on plans for our next visit."

All but the most controlling or very needy patients will gracefully accept one of these maneuvers. Still, ending an appointment on time can present a challenge. There is always the temptation to give the patient some extra time.

USING SPECIFIC QUESTIONS TO HELP THE PATIENT FOCUS ON DIAGNOSTIC MATERIAL

Making the primary *Diagnostic and Statistical Manual of Mental Disorders* (DSM-IV) congruent diagnosis (or diagnoses) on initial contact with the patient is the biggest favor a clinician can do for the patient. In a limited time frame, one is also always checking for chemical abuse and dependency that often "flies in under the radar." Indeed, as the sessions unfold, one should anticipate adding other Axis I co-morbid diagnoses as well as Axis II personality disorders. For whatever reason, it may take several sessions before an Axis II disorder becomes totally obvious.

Patients will often begin their session by telling their painful story, mentioning as they go along the names of Axis I diagnoses that other clinicians have made (which may or may not be correct). Any such diagnostic data need to be checked against DSM-IV criteria.

Here are some shortcuts to help arrive at a specific diagnosis: "If they were going to give out medals for being a worrier, would you get a medal?" If answered affirmatively, this should open up a quick review of the six diagnostic symptoms of generalized anxiety disorder.

John Ewing, MD's, CAGE test for alcoholism, when asked in a sequence not probing about alcohol or substance use issues, uses a neutral but good question: "Have you ever felt you should cut down on your drinking?" This opens up the CAGE criteria for alcoholism: Cut down; Annoyed by anyone criticizing your drinking; ever felt bad or Guilty about your drinking, had a drink in the morning to steady your nerves or get rid of a hangover (Eye opener) (www.patient.co.uk/showdoc/40025275 to print out a form and its scoring).

The question "Do your moods seem to be on a roller coaster all the time?" opens up an exploration of rapid-cycling bipolar or borderline personality disorder.

"Are you shy?" opens up a discussion of social phobia disorder.

"Do you have panic attacks?" usually gets a quick response, and the text criteria from DSM-IV quickly confirms (but don't forget to ask how much caffeine is being ingested).

"Do you miss many days of work because you feel poorly and stay in bed or on the couch? When you feel bad do you feel like crying a lot?" These questions open up the conversation about criteria for severe depression.

"Do you get so angry that you break stuff up?" opens up the issue of intermittent explosive disorder, while "Have you been in jail or prison?" with a person who seems to have antisocial personality traits opens the way to inquire about that DSM-IV criteria. Surprisingly, many such patients seem to feel no stigma about spending time in an adult correctional institution.

USING PATIENT TIME TO FILL OUT FORMS

When the clinician receives forms by mail or fax, or when the patient brings in forms to be filled out, it is best to begin the session by saying:

Today we have a form to fill out that is important to your care, so let's begin by using this session together to make sure we get the information sorted out correctly. This way, we can also be sure it will be mailed in a timely manner. However, we may not have very much time left over to discuss other matters during this session.

For example, it is quite helpful to have the patient there while filling out Social Security Disability forms, since many of the questions deal with issues that may not come up routinely.

Letters to employers can also be dealt with in this manner, giving only the most "vanilla" information as is possible, for example:

TO: Whom It May Concern
FROM: FGG
SUBJECT: Return to Work
DATE: July 19, 2008

Ms. C.D. _____ (date of birth) has been unable to come to work since _____ because of a medical disorder. She currently is highly motivated to return to work and has been very cooperative in her treatment, and is now not quite ready to return to her job.

Since this letter is given to the patient (on letterhead that may or may not state clinical specialty), the patient does not have to sign a release of information form.

Don't forget to photocopy the communication for the patient's chart.

GETTING THE NOTE WRITTEN

Managed care organizations (MCOs) make many demands: documenting face time between the clinician and the patient, and writing a note that documents:

The patient's progress
Significant psychosocial changes
Some element(s) of the mental status
The type of therapy performed
The patient's response to the session

Medication management issues
Other patient management issues, particularly if complex

Obviously, the better the clinician documents these issues, the better the outcome of an audit, and the fewer dollars that will end up having to be returned to the MCO for failing to substantiate a claim. Moreover, being accused by the Center for Medicare and Medicaid Services (CMS) or an MCO of unnecessarily "upcoding" one's current procedural terminology (CPT) charges is no fun.

One solution to the face time/documentation dilemma is to write the note *with* the patient, and if not contraindicated (on psychodynamic grounds), reading all or at least parts of the note back to the patient. When using a computer screen for an electronic medical record, for many patients it is quite all right to turn the screen partially toward the patient, sitting to your side so that the patient can see the note writing. Then the process becomes transparent rather than opaque, and note writing becomes a collaborative activity.

MAXIMIZING USE OF FTK TIMES

Patients that did not keep appointment (DNKA) or fail to keep (FTK) it are a mixed blessing for the busy clinician. The lack of compliance may represent a chaotic lifestyle that no coaxing or coaching can change. At times an apt interpretation will help correct this "bad habit." But the threat of either having to pay for time that could not be rescheduled or being terminated will cut down somewhat on FTKs.

Part of this FTK time may be spent with a more thorough review of the missing patient's chart than would otherwise be likely. When patients are a few minutes late, they need to realize that they have short-changed themselves:

> I'm sorry you couldn't get here on time. I'm afraid we won't be able to make up that time. So, let's not use the minutes we do have to talk about the circumstances that made you late. Instead, let's just get to the issues about your medication and how you are responding to it.

During the time the patient is not yet present, one can also return telephone calls or catch up on the literature. Certainly when the patient is more tardy than half of the appointment time, the clinician can use that time for any purpose. It is always wise to send out a brief note to the FTK patient reminding him or her about the no-show policy (see Chapter 8). One good activity for the clinician when the patient is late or has an FTK is to take care of oneself by practicing a bit of relaxation/meditation. The 20-minute hour is felt by most clinicians to be far more stressful than the typical 50-minute hour.

USING MEASUREMENT TOOLS BEFORE, DURING, OR AFTER THE SESSION

As discussed in Chapter 2, the use of a Visual Analogue Scale (VAS) is one shortcut to determine how a patient is doing and feeling.

When a patient presents with depression or anxiety as a chief complaint, using a VAS is a "no-brainer."

But what should the clinician do when after six sessions, the patient mentions that he or she thinks his or her poor concentration and working memory might be due to attention-deficit disorder (ADD), inattentive type? For example, the 20-minute hour is half over. It is not unusual after the acute distress from a patient's depressive or anxiety disorder has been resolved, for the patient to raise the belief that he has attention-deficit disorder. Then one can say:

> Mr. E, that is a very interesting idea. Let's discuss it at our next session, where we'll try to make it a special focus. I will have a paper-and-pencil test that I can give you, a screening test, that may help us to clarify the issue.

The Adult Self-Report Scale (ASRS) Symptom Checklist for ADHD and ADD is put out by the World Health Organization. Of course, no 18-item paper-and-pencil test can make a diagnosis, but this test does have good sensitivity and specificity, and typically ADHD patients complete the brief questions in less than two or three minutes. Then the rest of the session or the next one can be devoted to psychoeducation and the explanation about a therapeutic medication trial.

In similar fashion, some patients, long after their initial intake, make known to the clinician their checking or other rituals.

Obviously, this raises the issue of obsessive compulsive disorder (OCD) as a co-morbid condition complicating the life of a patient, for example, with recurrent, nonpsychotic unipolar depressions.

A shortcut here is to give the patient the Y-BOCS Severity Ratings devised by Wayne Goodman, MD. An easy-to-administer form can be readily found (www.atlantapsychiatry.com/forms), as well as the YBOCS Symptoms Checklist (http://healthnet.umassmed.edu/ mhealth > forms), which can be very helpful. These very cautious OCD patients often take 5 to 15 minutes to complete one or both, so it is best to give the form to them and have them complete it in the waiting room after the session is complete, and then hand it in to the receptionist, to be scored and discussed at the next session.

To follow the course of severe depression, the Quick Inventory of Depressive Symptomatology, Self-Report (QIDS-SR) by A. J. Rush, MD, is a 16-item checklist that requires 15 to 20 minutes at most to complete, and could be done by the patient in the waiting room before the session. Its use by the patient is as satisfactory as the clinician-administered test, and the self-report form can be quickly scored by the clinician or a secretary (www.ids-qids.org for forms, scoring instructions, and comparison to the Hamilton and the MADRS).

The mood chart (daily ratings of depression and mania, a month at a time, by Gary Sachs, MD, at www.bipolar.org) allows the rapid-cycling or ultra-rapid-cycling bipolar patient to show graphically his or her mood variations that words alone can rarely describe. Brought in by the patient at each visit, the mood chart lists compliance, irritability, sleep, and other symptoms and occurrences. Patients with at least an average intelligence can be taught how to use such a scale in a minute or two.

The Mood Disorder Questionnaire of Robert Hirschfeld, MD (www.psycheducation.org/depression/MDQ.html) has 13 plus items that can help the clinician and patient tease out if the patient does indeed have bipolar illness (symptoms happen at the same time, present a moderate to serious problem, and score 7 or higher). But as with all paper-and-pencil tests, there can be false positives and false negatives. It takes five minutes or less to complete (see Chapter 10 for further details).

There are other brief self-rating scales that are good for use in the office, or around the time of the visit, to assist the clinician and the patient in following progress:

Social Phobia Inventory (J. Davidson)—17 items; http://healthnet. umassmed.edu/mhealth (forms with a score ≥19 differentiate those with the condition vs. normal controls, in *BJPsychiat* 176 (2000): 379–386).

Geriatric Depression Scale (J. A. Yesavage)—15 items; www. stanford.edu/~yesavage/GDS.english.short.score (score >5 points is suggestive of depression and >10 is almost always depression).

Beck Depression Inventory-II (A. Beck)—21 items, 5–10 minutes; may be a widely used assessment tool, but is not in the public domain, and costs about $2 for each test, available from Harcourt Assessment.

Abnormal Involuntary Movement Scale (AIMS)—14 items, 5 minutes; www.atlantapsychiatry.com/forms/AIMS.pdf

Having access to such data can be a great shortcut that is also very useful for patient care. All this web-based material and more is listed in the appendix.

While the patient is filling out the rating forms, the clinician can be writing up parts of the session, doing other paperwork, or writing prescriptions. Forms for specific patients can be given to them before the session begins (ask them to come in early), or forms can be filled out just after the session, reminding the patient to be sure to hand it in to the receptionist. Most patients do appreciate the opportunity to communicate accurately the severity of their specific symptoms. They also appreciate being able to see that progress has been made.

BUILDING YOUR OWN WEB PAGE

A benefit of for psychiatrists that are members of the American Psychiatric Association is the ability to create one's own web page, through www.medem.com, for $350 yearly. Medem is a firm that also has contracts with a number of other medical organizations. My Web site through Medem, www.guggenheim.yourmd.com, gets about 100 hits per month. The major advantage of using the site is the ability to put in place web links and recent references from the literature that one's patients can use for their education. Additionally, one can list one's curriculum vitae (CV), telephone numbers for messages, types of patients to be served by the practice, and philosophy of care, such as: "I braid together psychoactive medication, brief psychotherapy, and patient education in a partnership on your journey back to health."

In telling my patients about my Web site, I always point out that it is a basic Web site, not an e-mail site, and that I have decided not to take advantage of having it as an interactive site for e-mail to or from my patients.

PATIENT-FRIENDLY WEB SITES

Medline Plus is a National Library of Medicine–NIH-sponsored site that has many medications with an easy-to-navigate system that answers: Why is this medication prescribed? How should it be used? Are there special precautions? What should be done if a dose is skipped? What side effects are caused? What should be done in the case of an overdose? What are the brand names? Printouts about medications can be useful to give to patients. The Web site also provides links to other trusted medical web pages. Go to http://medlineplus.gov > Drugs and Supplements.

NIMH has a useful basic Web site for patients at www.nimh.nih.gov > Health and Outreach > Mental Health Topics. Similarly, NIDA and NIAAA have Web site information as well as pamphlet-type material for patients.

Some of the web links that patients often appreciate are to the National Institute of Mental Health (NIMH), National Depressive and Manic Depressive Association, National Alliance on Mental Illness (NAMI), Anxiety Disorders Association of America, Borderline Personality Disorder Resource Center, and Madison Institute of Medicine. For families interested in developmental disabilities and dual diagnoses, the Web site of the National Association of Dually Diagnosed is helpful.

USING EPOCRATES

The Web site www.epocrates.com that gives very useful information for ongoing psychiatric practice is readily downloadable to a Palm Pilot, easy enough to do even for the novice, technophobe prescriber. In addition, the site has a $50 annual subscription component, more useful for internists and pediatricians. Instead of having to get up from the desk to get a pharmacological text off the shelf and leaf through the index to find the psychotropic needed, a handy pocket digital assistant (PDA) can, within seconds, alert the prescriber to the brand and generic name, which formularies carry it, the relative extent of co-pay (tiers 1, 2, and 3), and its lowest wholesale cost (from www.drugstore.com). It also lists starting dosage, side effects, adverse responses, pregnancy risk (Class A, B, C, and D), and potential drug-drug reactions.

The $50 Web site of ePocrates also provides all of the above plus a photograph of the appearance of most of the brand name tablets and capsules, as well as some of the generics, too. This can help when the patient mentions that he or she was prescribed a little oblong brownish tablet in the emergency room last night that has had a marvelous impact on the manic symptoms (although one has to choose which medications to look up on the Web site, as there is no site yet for "tan or brown-colored psychoactive medication").

PDR.net is free for U.S.-based physicians but requires registration and, like ePocrates, has a PDA version for drugs and their interactions.

ALGORITHMS

For online algorithms, the Texas Medication Algorithm Project is available at www.dhs.state.tx.us/mhprograms/TMAPtoc.shtm for depression, bipolar disorder, and schizophrenia. Disorders and anxiety in patients with substance abuse are covered at http://mhc.com/Algorithms. The International Psychopharmacology Project covers depression, schizophrenia, PTSD, and generalized anxiety disorder.

The American Psychiatric Association (www.psych.org) makes available for downloading practice guidelines under "Psychiatric Practice."

DOING SEARCHES ON THE WEB

Almost every computer-literate person knows how to Google, as well as the benefits of www.Ask.com. There are many other good Web sites aimed more at academicians and clinicians. For broad searches with some free access to journals, see www.highwire.stanford.edu and the National Library of Congress with its www.pubmed.gov.

Other good sites are www.searchmedica.com/psychiatry and www.medscape.com/psychiatry. Another site is www.psychiatric-times.com.

For drug interactions of the cytochrome P 450 system there is Indiana University's http://medicine.iupui.edu/flockhart/table.htm.

Free psychiatric rating scales for depression, such as the Patient Health Questionnaire-9 (PHQ-9), are available at www.depression-primarycare.org/clinicians/toolkits/materials/forms/phq9.

USING HANDOUT MATERIAL
FOR PSYCHOEDUCATION

A number of organizations have handouts that are very patient-friendly. Some of the outstanding organizations with helpful paper reading material are:

National Alliance for the Mentally Ill (www.nami.org)
National Depressive and Manic Depressive Association
    (www.ndmda.org)
Anxiety Disorders Association of America (www.adaa.org)
Obsessive Compulsive Foundation (www.ocfoundation.org)
National Institutes of Health (www.nimh.nih.gov)
Massachusetts General Hospital (www.bipolar.org)
Madison Institute of Medicine (www.miminc.org)
Trichotillomania Learning Center, Inc. (www.trich.org)
American Psychiatric Association (www.psych.org)

Peer support groups, through NAMI, NDMDA, AA, Al Anon, ACOA, CA, and NA, are often wonderful sources of assistance to patients in their quest for wholeness and healthful living.

RESTOCKING SUPPLIES WEEKLY,
SO AS TO NOT RUN OUT

This suggestion is not rocket science, but running out of prescription pads, appointment cards, lined writing paper, laboratory requisition slips, or release of information slips is irksome; not having a copy of the formulary that manages the patient's medication benefits can disrupt an otherwise smooth-running operation.

AVOIDING MALPRACTICE WORRIES

No matter how pressed one is for time, there are some simple rules to follow to avoid having to worry about malpractice issues. Even the best, brightest, and most diligent clinicians can occasionally have bad luck befall a patient that might hint of less than diligent care unless you have protected yourself. Nationwide a claim is filed against 7% of psychiatrists each year, with suicide and attempted suicide the most frequently cited causes of liability payments. The Psychiatrists' Professional Risk Management Program makes recommendations relevant to outpatient care (Table 6.1).

No one can document everything perfectly all the time, but failure to do this on a persistent basis is playing Russian roulette with plaintiff's lawyers. It is far easier to develop good documentation habits earlier than later.

LETTING THE RECEPTIONIST SCHEDULE THE PATIENT'S RETURN VISIT

On a tight schedule, such as a 20-minute hour, one had best not use the 1 to 5 minutes required to set up the next specific appointment. Telling the patient "one week," "four weeks," or "three months" is in everyone's interest. Then a book of times available to the receptionist with appointment cards completes the process. These appointment cards can serve as wonderful visual cues and reminders if placed in some highly visible place, like on the refrigerator door, held by a magnet. Although reasons why a patient can or cannot come at a particular time are always interesting, they rarely contribute additional information to a further understanding of the patient's condition. Forgetful patients forget, chaotic patients can't get a ride, and occasionally conscientious patients get bogged down.

Table 6.1 How to Avoid Malpractice Problems

1.	Document ongoing monitoring and evaluation of suicidality.
2.	Respond to family members' calls about a patient's suicidality; returning calls to hear their concerns is all right; releasing information to them without explicit permission, unless there is imminent danger, is not all right.
3.	Inquire about and document access to firearms and other dangerous weapons.
4.	Warn a third party when a dangerous patient has identified that party as a victim.
5.	Obtain permission to discuss the patient's condition with an involved psychotherapist, and do not assume that the psychotherapist will call you in case of the patient's deteriorating clinical condition.
6.	For patients on lithium, document levels plus kidney and thyroid function.
7.	For all medications, have some type of documentation that the patient is an informed consumer knowing the risks, benefits, and alternatives (R/B/A), especially with off-label usage.
8.	Document what medications and changes in dosage have been ordered and the indication.
9.	Document even the obvious clinical rationale for a treatment plan.
10.	Get immediate legal counsel when there is a subpoena to provide patient records or to testify.
11.	Do not let the suicidal patient become lost to follow-up.
12.	Do not send a patient's overdue bill to collection without reviewing the chart and speaking to the patient about it.
13.	Do not provide partial free care that falls below the level of your standard care.
14.	Do not allow patients to pay off their bill through personal services.
15.	Do not ignore steps on the clinician–patient termination process.
16.	Do not terminate summarily a patient in crisis.
17.	Do not fail to establish a record for a patient who is a VIP or has very sensitive material to discuss.
18.	Do not alter a patient record after an adverse event.
19.	Do not become sexually involved with a patient or former patient.

Chapter 7

Early and Later Pitfalls

Pitfalls in patient care can happen when patients are seen for 50 minutes, for 20 minutes, or for less time than that. However, with more patients to see per day and less time to see them, there are more opportunities for errors of omission or commission. Diagnostic and documentation errors seem more likely to occur when one doesn't know the patient as well, there are more time pressures, and there is less time for reflection. Having a prompt sheet for items to cover on the initial intake does seem to help.

PITFALLS IN INTERVIEWING THE PATIENT

Patients often expect their clinician to understand personal or medical issues that they haven't fully explained. Some may impute powers of comprehension that are not there without further communication. Patients also at times use ordinary medical terminology infused with special meanings or their own idiosyncratic terminology, and expect the clinician implicitly will understand. An obvious error may result from accepting the patient's terminology uncritically. For example, a hypomanic patient may say that he is having a "normal" or "good" day, when he is actually speeding, spending, and gambling. Many patients may deny they are "depressed" but agree that they feel sad, blue, hopeless, lonely, or down.

Some clinicians talk over their patients' heads, not mindful of the obtuseness of their lingo for the patient. A surprising number of internists and surgeons are particularly good at using highly technical terminology. Only the brightest patients can understand their illness at a physiological and molecular level; the majority of patients want a very simple schema that can be readily understood and remembered well enough to tell their loved ones. When a supervisor is able to observe communication between patient and trainee, it is not uncommon to see the trainee and patient each talking past the other, rather than with each other, when it comes to explaining the causation of the patient's illness and the mechanism of action of corrective treatment.

RELATIONSHIP PITFALLS

Sad patients usually don't match well with very enthusiastic clinicians, so it is incumbent on the clinician to titrate this personal characteristic. Another conflict is the patient seeking autonomy and the therapist invoking his or her authority. Emphasis on partnership in care sidesteps this issue.

COUNTERTRANSFERENCE PITFALLS

A health care partnership often requires a delicate balance between the clinician's impulse to be authoritarian and the patient's wish to be autonomous. Showing one's irritability or frustration is rarely a good idea. The clinician should, however, indicate to the patient when the patient is making an inappropriate decision. For example, when that decision is about discontinuing a medication, which would be contrary to the best interests of care, one might say:

> Mr. F, I disagree with your decision about the medication, but it is your body and you need to be the boss of you [assuming the patient is not suicidal, homicidal, or gravely disabled]. I am your coach, and it's my responsibility to let you know that I think you are making a mistake.

Nonetheless, the prescriber may well have strong feelings about the matter.

Patients with diagnoses of Axis II personality disorders are often more vexing to some clinicians than those with other conditions. There are also other patients that bring up a flood of feelings and associations due to the clinician's own personal prior traumatic experiences. As long as the clinician doesn't essentially "tune out" for more than 20 seconds, all is probably OK. But if the clinician is "off duty" while "on duty," he or she must deal with his or her personal issues if he or she is going to give responsible care to that patient.

DIAGNOSTIC PITFALLS

It's generally easy to make a diagnosis of major depressive disorder. The acronym SIG: E CAPS always helps (sleep, interest, guilt, energy, concentration, appetite for food and sex, psychomotor retardation or agitation, suicidal or homicidal ideation). Really depressed patients often reek of depression. But sometimes that depression is of the bipolar rather than the unipolar type. Unless one specifically probes for subtle, perhaps long-past episodes of energy spurts, it is quite easy to miss the bipolar component. About one in four patients presenting with depression may be misdiagnosed as unipolar rather than bipolar depressed.

Some clinical clues pointing to possibility of bipolar disorder: a family history of bipolar disease, hypersomnia rather than the insomnia of major depression, a prior episode of postpartum depression, and the presence of several co-morbid psychiatric conditions. Bipolar disorder is a diagnosis that is often missed, because when depleted and depressed as their history is being taken, these patients don't often think back spontaneously to their hyperaroused or euphoric times (see Chapter 10).

A survey of the membership of the National Depressive and Manic Depressive Association revealed that, on average, it took 10 years in the mental health system for the diagnosis of depression to be changed to bipolar with depression or mixed state. So this surely fits the criterion of a frequent error of omission, which can often be rectified, if one remembers to do it, by reading the patient the diagnostic criteria for hypomania from *Diagnostic and Statistical Manual of Mental Disorders* (DSM-IV) or administering Hirschfeld's Mood Disorder Questionnaire, a screening instrument for bipolar disorder. The detection of this disorder in a currently depressed patient can often be done in less than five minutes, entirely doable during the 20-minute hour (see Chapter 10).

A frequent diagnostic omission is that of generalized anxiety disorder or one of the other anxiety disorders, when the chief complaint and most important historical features relate to a severe affective disorder. Adequate reimbursement for hospital admissions may soon hang on the detection of co-morbid conditions.

And good patient care dictates that the clinician fully understand all the psychiatric conditions that impact the patient's plight.

Another diagnostic omission is the neglect of a co-morbid Axis II personality disorder. Given that more than 20% of the population has at least one such diagnosis, then certainly there must be at least this much Axis II psychopathology among patients with Axis I disorders such as depression or panic disorder. Typically Axis II pathology creeps into the awareness of the clinician after the first few visits. Then the clinician can haul out, with explanation, a well-used copy of DSM-IV.

> Mr. G, there may be an aspect of your personality type that may help us to understand why you have been having problems on the job, not just in the past six months, but for many years. This is a copy of the American Psychiatric Association's handbook on psychiatric diagnoses. So let's go over one of the criteria sets to see whether or not it seems to fit the kinds of difficulties that you have been having.

The importance of knowing if the patient has an Axis II disorder, and if so, what type, is that it gives the clinician more insight into ongoing behaviors plus potential transference and countertransference issues.

Still another diagnostic omission that is common is a co-morbid substance abuse problem, when the patient doesn't see use of substances as a problem, and indeed may see substances as part of the solution. Patients don't tend to talk about material that is ego-syntonic, rather just things that are ego-dystonic.

DETRIMENTAL OMISSION OF CERTAIN DETAILS

Lethality often fluctuates across the course of an affective illness. An inquiry on the initial diagnostic intake should put this important information in an easy-to-find place, should the patient's condition suddenly take a turn for the worse. Lethality can be rapidly self-rated by the patient as can depression, hypomania, and anxiety (see Chapter 2).

Compliance with other physicians on issues of adherence to medication regimens or with attendance to appointments is important information, useful to have when developing an initial contract with the patient.

Inquiry about possibly being pregnant, the constancy of use of contraception, and what type of contraception is used becomes particularly important when one is prescribing medications that are from Class D, particularly Depakote, which is (potentially) quite toxic to fetuses. Responses to these questions need to be documented. Benzodiazepines such as Xanax or Ativan can be teratrogenic early in pregnancy, especially in the weeks before the patient even realizes that she is pregnant, so taking and recording a contraceptive history of all females from ages 9 to 50 is really necessary, while informing them that if they wish to get pregnant or not use contraception, this issue needs to be discussed well in advance to protect the fetus (see Chapter 22).

Another potential hazard for female patients is the use of psychotropic drugs that increase enzymatic metabolism of other medications: For example, oxcarbazepine (Trileptal) or carbamazepine (Tegretol) can speed up the hepatic degradation of birth control pills, lowering effective levels such that unwanted pregnancies can occur unless a greater strength of birth control pill is used for contraception. It's quite easy to get a pregnancy test on patients being admitted to a psychiatric unit, as a way of avoiding a painful complication when using any psychotropic medication.

Covert intimate partner violence is another important condition that is often identified, but only if one asks. Many patients are reluctant to bring this up on their own initiative. Another simple piece of information that is easy to omit is the presence of homicidal ideation. Clinicians reflexively inquire about suicidal ideation in an initial workup, but homicidal ideation is often omitted because it is apparently far more rare. But psychiatric patients do harbor such thoughts, and inattention to them can be a costly omission.

DOCUMENTATION PITFALLS

When one is charging for a time-sensitive CPT procedure, such as psychiatric consultation on the general medical floor, the omission of the times of starting and stopping a psychiatric consultation, for example, can result in a major downcoding by the managed care organization (MCO). If this turns up in a formal audit, where 1 of 25 randomly chosen charts is missing these data, the consequences to a provider or an institution can result in many thousands of dollars being recouped by the auditing organization (Medicare, MCO, etc.).

Another pitfall is the lack of a statement in the record that the prescriber has talked to the patient about the risks, as well as the benefits, of starting a new medication. Even simple and common medications like aspirin can be toxic, and typically 10 to 40 people per year die from taking that medication. For example, there is hardly a medication currently in use for the treatment of bipolar disorder that cannot, for a very few unfortunate patients, have very adverse consequences. Thus, include a statement in the chart such as: "We have discussed the risks and benefits of the medication regimen, and I feel that the patient is making an informed choice."

Better yet would be to add what some of the risks are, for example, tardive dyskinesia, Stevens-Johnson syndrome, renal insufficiency, hypothyroidism. If the prescriber feels, in his or her professional judgment, that it is improper at the present time to discuss such issues with the patient because of the clinical condition, this too should be documented. Although psychiatrists are sued far less than physicians in other specialties, one does not want to open up himself or herself to adversity from a disgruntled family member.

PITFALLS IN MANAGING THE SERIOUSLY SUICIDAL PATIENT

The biggest problem in trying to care for a suicidal patient is knowing how to judge the extent of the patient's lethality. Obviously, being aware of the issue and documenting it are important, but measuring the patient's lethality, *with the patient,* before the patient has entered a help repudiation phase, is very helpful. Ask the patient: "On a scale of 0% to 100%, where 0% means not suicidal at all and 100% means you are about to do it, how suicidal are you now?"

The biggest pitfalls are:

1. Not asking about the patient's lethality. (Research has proven that this does not plant such ideas in a patient's mind).
2. Not asking if there is a firearm with ammunition in the home. If it is impossible to remove all firearms from the house, at least all bullets can be removed.

3. Not keeping in touch with the family and an involved mental health worker, should there be a life-threatening crisis.

Although there may be HIPPA issues involved, the patient's right to privacy can be waived in emergency situations. But before anything untoward occurs, if one has a very high-risk outpatient, it is always wise to carry on a 3 × 5 inch card, or in a password-protected section of one's Palm Pilot, important and readily accessible information about the patient, such as telephone numbers of the patient and significant others, plus other identifying information (see Chapter 21).

SERVICE PITFALLS

This is the era of the service industry, and clinicians render some of the most intimate of all services. There is an expectation that telephone calls to a prescriber be returned within one business day. If an entitled but not seriously suicidal patient's telephone calls are becoming burdensome, however, that issue, and what are appropriate limits, needs to be addressed at the next office session (see Chapter 3). One might consider some variation of the following:

> Miss H, I understand that you may feel the need to check in with me several times a day, and are feeling entitled to talk with me. But that is not how I can run my busy practice. So if we are to work together as partners, you must only call me if you feel you are dangerously suicidal. Otherwise, you must limit your communications to those times when I am evaluating you and your medication regimen in the office.

COMPLIANCE PITFALLS

Adherence to a medication regimen can be complicated for a variety of reasons. An easy way to inquire about this in a nonjudgmental fashion is asking the question: "How many pills do you think you missed last month?"

Other ways to accomplish this are requesting patients to bring in all their medications, and then doing a quick pill count. A third technique is checking with the pharmacist if the patient asks that one of his or her prescriptions be called in, to see whether refills have been used on a timely basis. Checking the medication flow sheet in the patient's medical record is also a potential screening tool for compliance: Has the patient asked for timely refills?

With patients that are given medication by a spouse because of confusion or unreliability, "cheeking" the medication can be avoided with rapidly dissolving tablets for clonazepam (Klonopin wafers), alprazolam (Niravam), mirtazepine (Remeron Sol Tab), olanzapine (Zyprexa Zydis), and others. Depot injections of some antipsychotics also increase adherence.

Using a daily clinical monitoring form, such as a mood-rating sheet for bipolar disorder, is another way of stressing the partnership and the importance of regularly taking medications as prescribed. The use of a pill minder, available at all pharmacies, is another way to avoid a compliance pitfall.

PITFALLS IN MEDICATING PATIENTS

It is important for the prescriber not to confuse medication regimens for depressed patients presenting for routine care for a mild–moderate depression with the regimen you would use for a patient that presents with an urgent need of care for a severe depression. With the former, the patient has a relatively mild degree of disability, and one can use monotherapy with a "start low, go slow" approach. With urgent care, one uses aggressive titration to effective dosage levels and quickly considers adding on adjunctive medications.

With patients that mention uncomfortable activation with a selective serotonin reuptake inhibitor (SSRI), the prescriber must be mindful that the patient may possibly be describing a switch from depression into hypomania. When antidepressants are prescribed, the patient needs to be warned of this possibility, and the need to discontinue the medication immediately, and then to call the prescriber immediately.

PITFALLS FROM MEDICATIONS REQUIRING SYSTEMATIC MONITORING

Clozapine is so potentially toxic that the Food and Drug Administration (FDA) has required weekly, then biweekly, white blood cell counts (WBCs) on all patients as part of the treatment plan, with compliance requirements no longer under the physicians' control. Other medications are not so potentially or frequently toxic, so they have been left for prescribers to monitor as they wish.

The monitoring of lithium levels, TSH, and creatinine levels is regularly subject to guidelines from different agencies and organizations. There is rather uniform agreement on semiannual monitoring of renal and thyroid parameters. There is not quite such uniformity about the frequency of lithium levels in either the newly started patient or the stable patient. The usually agreed upon standard is biweekly, then monthly, and then quarterly, as long as the patient has had relatively stable lithium levels that are neither too high nor too low.

Following the serum sodium in patients on oxcarbazepine is quite important on a monthly basis for the first quarter, and then quarterly afterwards, because of hyponatremia, although this parameter is often not followed so closely because of unfamiliarity with the frequency or symptoms of mild hyponatremia.

Carbamazepine and divalproexic both require CBCs and LFTs at least semiannually, but some institutions require more frequent monitoring. The prescriber that does not carefully monitor patients on these medications, or do liver function studies in patients on nefazodone (Serzone) or duloxetine (Cymbalta), is running a chance of falling into a large pit of trouble.

A predictable pitfall is weight gain in many, but not all, patients on such diverse medications as clozapine (Clozaril), olanzapine (Zyprexa), risperidone (Risperdal), quetiapine (Seroquel), lithium, divalproexic (Depakote), carbamazepine (Tegretol), tricyclics (Elavil, etc.), mirtazepine (Remeron), and paroxetine (Paxil), among others. Gaining four pounds in the initial month should be a major tip-off, and probably should call for a medication change if the patient gains eight pounds in two months. There are far too many psychiatric patients with 30- to 100-pound weight gains, gains that might have been avoided.

The metabolic syndrome, with increases in body mass index, abdominal girth, blood pressure, cholesterol, and blood sugar, has been addressed by numerous organizations, with diverse sets of guidelines about monitoring. To not follow some set of guidelines is bad for the health of the patient and the well-being of the prescriber following such a patient. It takes less than 30 seconds to have patients weigh themselves on the scale in the office and measure their girth (when handed a tape measure already pulled out to 35 or 40 inches). Baseline weights at 4, 8, and 12 weeks are important, as well as fasting blood sugar and lipid profile, to monitor their condition at baseline, 12 weeks, then as needed afterwards.

Less well publicized are the side effects of polycystic ovarian syndrome, with hirsutism, acne, obesity, amenorrhea or menstrual irregularities, and infertility, which has been associated with the use of Depakote, among other drugs.

PITFALLS IN TRYING TO GET ALL JOINT COMMISSION ON ACCREDITATION OF HEALTH CARE ORGANIZATIONS (JCAHO)-REQUIRED DOCUMENTATION ON THE FIRST VISIT

Some accreditation agencies require a wealth of information, including details about physical and sexual abuse, spiritual orientation, social history, and family history of mental and drug/alcohol abuse. Although all such information is relevant, few clinicians will be able to "fill in all the blanks" on the first visit, or even the first few visits in a very complex patient, except in extraordinary circumstances (a patient with a very simple and short history and an uncomplicated life).

In such instances, a simple solution is to just write "deferred" in a slot for this information. Then one can revisit the initial intake note at subsequent visits and complete the required documentation. A yellow highlighter applied to "deferred" is a good prompt to follow up on such an item on a subsequent occasion.

PITFALLS INVOLVING MANAGED CARE ORGANIZATIONS

Books have been written about clinicians' grievances concerning MCOs. Unless one refuses to accept insurance, MCOs can't be avoided. Moreover, one will come to grief unless one plays by the rules that they set up, and each company has its own way of playing the game. Being nice to the reviewer on the telephone can work wonders: You catch more flies with honey than with vinegar.

A less frequently considered pitfall of doing business with MCOs is relying too heavily on any one company. It is time-consuming to fill out applications to be on an MCO panel, and the waiting period for a successful clinician applicant to be credentialed often varies from two to six months. But relying on just one or two companies can be devastating to income if one company decides suddenly to decrease the size of its panel, or decides to cease doing business in a particular state.

PITFALLS OF SPLIT THERAPY

In an era where MCOs' reimbursement schema encourage split therapy, there still remains the standard of frequent communication between psychiatrist and psychotherapist. In a busy practice, this tradition is often regarded more in the breach than in practice. Although often such direct communication is not vital to adequate care, there certainly can be instances in which the patient comes to grief because of lack of communication. When a borderline patient engages in splitting, when there are compliance or drug abuse issues, when potential suicide or homicide threats come up, the all too frequent inertia about communication needs to be put aside.

It is far easier to get a consent to communicate with the psychotherapist initially than at some later time when there is a complicating factor, such as noncompliance, suicidal or homicidal ideation, worsening depression, or severe side effects of medication.

Another impetus to communication of the prescriber with the psychotherapist (when the patient has split therapy) is a defensive one. Should the patient's outcome be tragic and the family sues, the plaintiff's attorney will reflexively seek "deeper pockets." Lawyers understand that collaborative care is rife with potential problems. Physicians typically carry more malpractice insurance. Even if the psychiatrist is totally blameless, it is often assumed that the physician is the "captain of the ship" (a situation that may have been true a decade ago, but is not necessarily true now). Moreover, the physician may have more impressive training and credentials than the other mental health clinicians, and thus may be felt to have more responsibility.

If the psychiatrist is seeing the patient for a one-time consultation at the behest of a psychotherapist or a primary care physician, it is important to document this fact in the chart to make clear that there is no continuing relationship.

Another example: If a prescriber is referred a patient for continuing medication management, and the prescriber is uncomfortable with some of that referring therapist's practices or belief systems, some prescribers would refer the patient back to the mental health worker for referral to another prescriber. This obviously is a complicated ethical issue, but does pose a potential problem in split therapy.

PITFALLS OF SOLO PRACTICE

Group practice, sharing an office with other clinicians, can do much to decrease the loneliness and isolation that solo practitioners experience.

Additionally, with troubling patients, informal curbstone consultations, as part of a group practice, can be quite helpful. Although some mental health workers other than psychiatrists continue to get supervision, psychiatrists rarely get formal supervision after residency.

Chapter 8

Terminating Treatment

THE PATIENT THAT TERMINATES YOU, FAILING TO SHOW UP

When the patient fails to show up for an initial appointment, should they be terminated, and if so, how? Those that fail to show up initially may do so because their acute problem has been in some way resolved. This often happens if the patient's appointment is more than 10 days after the initial call. Obviously, the sooner that one can see the patient, the more likely that it is close to the golden moment of need and openness to solution and change.

Another reason for an initial no-show is that the patient did not agree in the first place for the need for the referral to the mental health specialist. A third reason for a no-show of an initial appointment is that the patient is too impaired, in terms of brain function or massive psychosocial stressors, to be able to tend to the niceties of scheduling and appointments.

Given the lack of information that the clinician has about the initial no-show, it is best to have the secretary (1) call to find out what happened to cause the failure to attend, and (2) send out a letter reminding the patient that he or she has missed the initial appointment, and what needs to be done to reschedule another.

Those that fail to attend follow-up appointments tend to be rather impaired and a have a higher chance of subsequently being admitted to a psychiatric hospital. From a demographic perspective, no-show patients are more likely to be an ethnic minority, homeless, and in a lower socioeconomic group; to have major ongoing psychosocial stressors; or to live at a greater distance from the clinic. They also tend to be younger, not taking their psychiatric medication, and more likely to be substance users.

Should these patients be terminated for "noncompliance" after one or two no-shows? Different clinics have different rigid or flexible rules about this. Usually clinical considerations carry considerable weight in the decision about termination, but allowing patients with considerable Axis II personality disorder pathology to occupy much needed appointment space can certainly be considered dysfunctional for the clinic and enabling for the patient.

PLANNED AND UNPLANNED TERMINATIONS

There are two types of terminations: planned and unplanned. Planned terminations are certainly the ideal, but things don't always work out that way. Many patients improve considerably, especially as their medication "kicks in" after four or six weeks. Some studies have indicated that as many as 50% of patients fail to show up by the fourth appointment. Some patients, as they are reengaged in their former life, minimize that they had a major mental disorder and forget their appointment until after it has passed. Sometimes such lapses occur even in conscientious and psychologically healthy individuals not much used to doctor's appointments. Telephoning the patient the day before the appointment cuts down somewhat on this type of "did not keep appointment" (DNKA), but it does not eliminate it.

DNKAS CAN LEAD TO UNPLANNED TERMINATIONS

The typical DNKA rate in medical and psychiatric clinics runs from 20% to 40%. There is a large literature on the subject, focusing on successful efforts to lower the DNKA rate, but major efforts to eradicate the problem do not yield very impressive results, and overbooking for psychiatric patients doesn't seem appropriate, although the Henry Ford Hospital does this in the medical clinic and, of course, airlines do this, too. Seeing patients soon after their call for help and reminding the patient (by mail or telephone) about forthcoming appointments are the two most productive techniques to decrease the DNKA rate.

When DNKA patients were queried about why they missed their appointments, the reasons that emerged were: not understanding the clinic system structure, not feeling respected or understood, having to wait more than 10 weekdays for an initial appointment, and a referral by a primary care physician (PCP) whose enthusiasm for the consultation exceeded the patient's. Other causes for patients missing appointments include financial problems with the co-pay and failure to improve as quickly and as much as expected.

Unfortunately for the clinician, managed care companies do not pay for missed appointments. For psychiatrists who do not accept insurance, and require patients to pay at each visit, the loss of income can be made up (by the patient) if the patient has signed a note indicating his or her obligation to pay in full for missed appointments. Those who accept insurance, which include most community mental health centers and academic medical centers, however, have given up the practice of charging patients $10 to $25 for missed appointments: The bookkeeping efforts, the cost of repetitively mailing out bills, and the low rate of collections make billing for DNKAs financially not worth the effort.

DEALING WITH THE MISSED APPOINTMENT

Typically the conscientious and improving patient will make a major effort not to miss the next appointment. When a patient does miss an appointment in intensive psychotherapy, interpreting the resistance and the role of the unconscious in repressing unpleasant associations can be a useful approach. But in combined medication management and brief psychotherapy in the 20-minute hour, the prescriber usually chooses to deal with the slip of forgetting an appointment merely at face value, as simple forgetting. But it is wise to remind the patient, in a friendly but firm fashion, of the clinic's policy on DNKAs:

> Mr. I, I want to continue to work with you, but I must remind you of the clinic policy that if you miss two appointments or have late cancellations, you will be terminated, and I would not want that to happen. So a word to the wise.

Thus, time in the session after a missed appointment is most productively spent on "business as usual" issues rather than on elaborate excuses and defensiveness, which is rarely productive in the 20-minute hour. With time at a premium, it is important to focus on critical issues such as residual symptoms of, for example, depression, if any; side effects of medication; cognitive restructuring issues; and educating the patient about his or her disorder and the length of time the patient needs to remain on the medication.

CANCELLATIONS CAN ALSO LEAD
TO UNPLANNED TERMINATIONS

When patients call the clinic secretary to cancel an appointment, the clinician does not know if this is the harbinger of a patient-generated termination, a manifestation of the patient's ambivalence about treatment, the result of a transference issue that needs to get resolved before further psychotherapeutic work can continue, or just that the patient's child is at home with the chicken pox and sitters are not available. It becomes very important that the clinician's receptionist taking the cancellation message understand the importance of inquiring further about why the appointment is being cancelled. Some prescribers instruct their receptionist:

> Please find out from the patient if he or she is better and is wishing to get further psych meds from the PCP. Or if the patient is cancelling because the medication has produced some undesirable side effects. Or is he or she dissatisfied with treatment? Or has there been a personal or health calamity? The patient should be asked if he or she wishes to reschedule the upcoming appointment for an opening that is more convenient? Or does the patient wish to call back later at a more convenient time to reschedule an appointment?

It is also important that the receptionist be instructed to record all these details and also the telephone numbers and times when the canceling patient can be reached by the clinician so as to increase the likelihood that the therapeutic relationship will continue to be ongoing, if appropriate.

Sometimes terminations just happen unintentionally. The patient cancels for a personally important reason and then the inertia of remaking the next appointment, with some procrastination, leads to ending an otherwise potentially productive relationship.

THE CHARACTEROLOGICALLY CHAOTIC PATIENT

Some patients cancel on short notice or fail to keep appointments on a regular basis. Such patients usually have strong Axis II pathology. They may be chaos prone or self-defeating. They certainly can be the bane of any clinician for a variety of reasons. Frequently missed appointments decrease the clinician's charges for the day. Just as important, such empty hours mean access to the clinician's schedule for other patients in need of treatment is blocked during that time.

Fortunately, there is some protection for the clinician from frequent DNKAs. All patients should have signed a patients' responsibility form, which indicates what is expected of the clinician and the clinic, and what is expected of the patient. Among the patient's responsibilities is to pay all their co-pays in a timely fashion and to keep appointments or cancel with 24 (or 48) hours' notice. According to this document, failure on the part of the patient to conform to this standard of practice on two (or three) such occasions within six months may be cause for termination.

Some frequent DNKA patients, leading chaotic lives, may eventually learn that their treatment needs cannot be assessed and treated without their active cooperation and collaboration. Although one would like to be available to all patients within the constraints at least of office hours, some patients' psychopathology makes them unable to conform to reasonable standards. If not in a highly lethal state, they should be sent termination notices. Such notices should be sent by registered mail, with a duplicate copy by regular mail (some people are not willing to sign for registered mail). Here the termination is not planned by the patient but *is* planned by the clinician. Such patients unfortunately end up being treated just by their PCPs with walk-in appointments, or by hospital emergency rooms and urgent care clinics.

WHEN THE TERMINATION IS MUTUAL

Fortunately, most patients do keep their appointments, and do improve. So when, for example, they are euthymic and in remission, when their anxiety is considerably lowered most of the time, or when their life crisis is resolved or resolving, a scheduled termination would seem to be in order. Thus, termination can be mutual, and even can be seen as a graduation of sorts, augmenting self-esteem. Some patients terminate because of forced or voluntary geographic moves. Still others are improved and, with some advance preparation, can be told that they are ready for graduation with no more need for treatment at this time, and that the clinician is pleased that the patient has had such a good outcome.

By the time patients are ready for termination they ought to have a good cognitive map of their disorder(s), and an understanding of what constitutes the need for intermittent or continued treatment, as the clinical case dictates. They should also know about available educational resources, including approved Web sites, suggested literature, and peer support groups.

If the improved patient will continue to need medication, it is important to remember that not all referring PCPs are ready and willing to accept that patient back into their practice for medication management, so in such a situation, termination is not practicable. This is particularly the case for patients with affective disorders on three or more psychoactive medications, or on psychoactive medications that most PCPs are not familiar with. Moreover, a small percentage of PCPs do not want to treat patients requiring any psychotropic medications at all.

For other patients that are improving, termination needs to have a different cast, since it is not a celebration, but rather a loss of a significant object and a source of stability. Such patients may need to be told that they can come back whenever they need to.

TERMINATION FOR PATIENTS THAT ARE NOT IMPROVING OR ARE GETTING WORSE

Some patients, lamentably, do not improve on intermittent scheduled outpatient treatment, even with multiple medication trials, including the use of various augmentation strategies. Here the options are complicated. One option is referral to a partial hospitalization program, assuming the patient is not seriously suicidal, dangerous, or gravely disabled. Emerging data show that remarkable improvement is usually the case for these (mostly) five-working-day programs. Insurance companies are usually willing to allow such treatment to stave off a far more expensive inpatient hospitalization.

Another option for the patient not improving or getting worse is referral to, or consultation with, another psychiatrist. But before partial hospitalization or referral to some other clinician, one must be certain that the patient is actually taking the correct amount of medication, that there is no covert issue with alcohol or substance abuse, and that the patient is being treated for the proper diagnosis.

WHAT TO DO WITH TREATMENT-REFRACTORY DEPRESSION (TRD)

A large number of patients with refractory depression, for example, actually do not have unipolar depression. Patients with bipolar II disorder, on average, are treated in the mental health system for ten years, with multiple drug trials and medications "pooping out" before the correct diagnosis is made. Moreover, a small proportion of depressed patients, perhaps 1%, have active thyroid pathology resulting in their depression. Perhaps that 1% chance was sitting undetected in your office today?

Another reason for nonimprovement may be that the patient has not been taking a full therapeutic dose as prescribed, despite pro-testations that he or she is doing so. There are a variety of reasons that can account for such potentially unexpected behavior: cost of high co-pays for medications, forgetfulness, or even the wish to continue in the sick roll.

How can one check on possible noncompliance? If the patient tends to be forgetful, find out if a pill minder is being used. One can also request that the patient bring all his or her medications into the office and then do a formal or informal pill count. Additionally, one can check the patient's medication refill sheet to examine the frequency of ordered refills. At times it can even be helpful, with permission, to talk tactfully with a pharmacist at the patient's drug store to help resolve this issue.

Another reason for lack of improvement is that the patient, unbeknownst to the clinician, has been abusing alcohol or illicit substances, taking large amounts of herbals, or getting a large supply of benzodiazepines from a PCP. All these matters should be explored before sending the patient elsewhere for more psycho-pharmacologic expertise.

SUMMARY

Terminations can be planned or otherwise. Unless anticipated, a surprisingly high proportion of cases "do not end with a bang, but with a whimper," merely drifting away, at times improved rather than in remission, at other times not improved at all. It is good practice to try to have planned terminations with all patients, but this will be a challenge.

For the busy clinician with a day full of back-to-back appointments, a DNKA can be a relief. But it is usually not an omen of a good outcome.

Part 2

Quick-Grab Chapters

Chapters 9 to 26 present the reader with a few pages of clinical orientation to help prepare for a specific clinical encounter and situations.

This primer does not claim to be encyclopedic, and not all clinical conditions are covered here. Rather, each of the quick-grab chapters stands alone, so that the clinician can read it in a few minutes. Each chapter is designed to inform the clinical encounter on topics such as the pregnant patient, the suicidal patient, and the angry patient.

Although almost all mental health clinicians think of themselves as both caring and intrepid, we do put ourselves very close to being in harms' way in professional situations that, in our personal lives and without our professional training, would often send us fleeing. Small portions of that primordial fear still persist, to be quieted with a centering in basic knowledge about what to expect and what to do. The last three chapters address issues that routinely make the clinician uncomfortable, but that need to be dealt with.

This is an era of rapid turnover in patients and ready access to references. In addition to widely publicized textbooks and journals, there are Internet search engines and well-vetted Internet sites providing a plethora of information. The appendix to this primer provides leads to further information on important clinical matters, with suggested readings that are quite up to date (November 2008).

The reader is encouraged to copy a chapter here and there to share with a colleague. Teaching and learning is a collaborative process, and this primer is intended to be a part of that.

Chapter 9

Working With the Depressed Patient

In this quick-grab chapter, we discuss diagnosis and treatment of the depressed patient. What would you want to bet that the next patient you evaluate will have a depression? That is, what are the odds? Table 9.1 outlines some diagnostic data from a private practice group that Ricky Akins, MD, and others compiled. He works with a private practice group of 36 adult and child psychiatrists, 34 therapists, and 45 nurses in 11 offices. The practice covers a pool of 1 million individuals from rural, suburban, and urban settings in Alabama.

So if you bet money that the next patient you see will have a depression as the primary psychiatric diagnosis, the odds are slightly in your favor. If that patient does meet criteria for major depressive disorder, based on the Baltimore ECA study of first episodes of depression with decades of follow-up, the chances of the patient never having another episode of major depression are about 50%,

Table 9.1 DSM-IV Diagnostic Spectrum in a Psychiatric Private Practice

Diagnosis	Percent of Population
Major depressive disorder, recurrent	30.4%
Major depressive disorder, single episode	12.2
Depressive disorder, not otherwise specified	6.3
Dysthymic disorder	2.5
Anxiety disorders	14.7
Substance use disorders	4.2
Adjustment disorder	8.4
Other	21.3
Total	100.0%

Source: Oepen, G. et al. (2006) *Psychiatric Times, 23,* 7.

with 15% having an unremitting course and 35% having recurrent episodes over the years.

DIAGNOSTIC ISSUES

When encountering a depressed patient, it is crucial to find out if the patient is having an adjustment disorder or a major depressive episode. Keeping a patient in traditional supportive therapy for a supposed adjustment disorder denies proper and effective treatment, if the patient actually has a major depressive disorder. Using the SIG: E CAPS mnemonic, as previously discussed (Chapter 1, p. 12), should help with sorting out this differential diagnosis.

This same mnemonic should also apply to bipolar depressed patients, although the pharmacological treatment is far different. For further discussion of differences in symptoms and in the history of bipolar versus unipolar depression, see Chapter 10, pp. 97–99. The important point is that many of these depressed patients will need medication management or cognitive behavioral therapy, or preferably both. Robert Hirschfeld, MD, has published an easy-to-use rapid screening questionnaire for the hypomanic symptoms of bipolar disorder (Chapter 10, p. 98). Many clinicians now do not start a severely depressed patient on an antidepressant without using such a screen, as it is easy to miss the bipolar part of a serious depressive episode.

Depressions that don't neatly fit into the category of a major unipolar depression or bipolar depression may have a subsyndromal affective disorder or some other type of disorder, including medical disorders such as thyroid, parathyroid, pancreatic, connective tissue, lung, blood, or neurological disorders that require specific rule-out diagnostic tests. Or they may be depressed because of an antihypertensive, a steroid, or another medication. Some patients that do fit into the criteria for a major depressive episode may also have a medical etiology or precipitant for the depression, so it is always best to medically screen each depressed patient. Moreover, just because a patient fits diagnostic criteria for major depressive disorder doesn't mean that he or she doesn't have a co-morbid general medical condition that the patient may or may not be aware of.

THE IMPACT OF RECURRENT MAJOR DEPRESSION

The impact of recurrent major depressive episodes impacts on many domains. There is poor functioning in the workplace and with the family, increased familial burden, worsened prognosis for established medical conditions, shortened life span, increased health care costs (mental and physical), increased likelihood of substance abuse, and increased likelihood of subsequent episodes if the current episode has a moderate response to medication.

Detection and prevention of suicide are important issues in the care of the depressed patient. Although only a portion of patients with depression are being treated for their depression when they commit suicide, still 90% of patients that commit suicide had seen a physician within a month of their death. (Measuring depression and suicidality is covered in Chapter 2. The suicidal patient is covered in Chapter 21.)

Depression is prevalent but not widely diagnosed in primary medical care. Even when it is treated, antidepressant medication is usually not prescribed in adequate doses. A research telephone community survey in Arkansas of adults determined that only a third of depressed patients who acknowledged symptoms of clinical depression in the research interview had been so diagnosed by their primary care physician. Of those that were being treated, only one-third were treated in adequate doses of antidepressants.

PATHOGENESIS OF MAJOR DEPRESSIVE DISORDER

Geneticists have known for the past five years that individuals with the short variant of the serotonin transporter gene (5-HTTLPR) experienced higher levels of depression and suicidality following recent life stressors. A small, and not yet replicated, study had non-depressed seven-year-old children with and without the short gene variant of the serotonin transporter participate; they were shown sad movie clips or asked to imagine a sad experience. Those children that were homozygous for 5-HTTLPR showed greater negative processing than did the other children.

Aaron Beck, the psychoanalyst who invented cognitive behavioral therapy, links this biasing of information processing to a propensity to develop depression. Moreover, he then links these findings to those from functional brain imaging, with often noted amygdala hyperactivity in depression. Recent research has also tied the 5-HTTLPR variant carrier to this hyperactivity. Putting the pieces together, he writes:

> Hyperactivity of the amygdala in the short 5-HTTLPR variant carriers is associated with increased sensitivity to negative stimuli and leads to negative bias in the processing or interpretation of emotional stimuli. Since the amygdala is involved in the evaluation and storage of emotionally charged events, its hyperactivity to negative stimuli in predisposed individuals would appear to represent a neurophysiological correlate of cognitive bias. (Beck 2008, p. 973)

THE ROLE OF COGNITIVE THERAPY

For the nonpsychotically depressed patient, and for the patient without melancholic or severe depression, cognitive behavioral therapy (CBT) and interpersonal therapy (ITP) both have important primary or adjunctive treatment roles. Recurrence rates are often lower when cognitive behavior therapy is involved than for patients just on medication. Numerous research studies have demonstrated that psychopharmacology and therapy are superior to just pharmacology alone.

STAR*D AND OTHER APPROPRIATE TREATMENT TRIALS OF DEPRESSION

A number of industry-supported pharmaceutical trials of individuals recruited for treatment paint a rather rosy picture of response (response defined as having 50% improvement on Hamilton Depression Rating Scales) or remission. For such trials, considerably less than half of applicants usually qualify, since subjects selected for treatment must be free of concurrent co-morbid psychiatric and medical conditions. But for those that volunteer for drug studies, results are often very encouraging. For example, a 12-week mirtazepine (Remeron) study showed 70% response rate, including 60% remission. Similarly, a 12-week sertraline (Zoloft) trial showed an 80% response rate, including a 43% remission rate, while a 12-week imipramine trial showed a 67% response rate, including a 41% remission rate.

But sponsored pharmaceutical trials with volunteer subjects do not usually represent the reality of patients seen in clinical practice. Patients in clinical practice often have a multitude of psychiatric and medical disorders and treatment-resistant depression, that is, depression that may respond to medication but does not go into remission. To remedy this situation, the NIMH sponsored the STAR*D trial to determine preferred treatments for depression truly representative of those patients seen in an ordinary clinical practice.

From 1999 to 2006, STAR*D enrolled 4,011 nonpsychotically depressed patients aged 18 to 75 who were already in 18 primary care and 23 psychiatric care settings and who had a Hamilton Rating Scale for Depression of at least 14 on the 17-item scale. A majority of patients had concurrent Axis I diagnoses. The patient cohort was on average 40 years of age with some college education; half had private insurance; a third had no insurance. Three-quarters of the group had recurrent depressions. Two-thirds had at least one concurrent medical condition. A third had had onset of depression before age 18. The mean duration of the depressive episode was 24 months, the duration of illness 15 years, and the mean Hamilton depression score was 22.

Treatment was open with randomization, but clinicians were guided by algorithms, supervision, and dose adjustments appropriate to achieve remission. Symptoms and side effects were measured at each visit, and there was active psychoeducation. Citalopram (Celexa) was the initial antidepressant chosen, the ultimate average dose slightly more than 40 mg, with duration of this phase of treatment at least 10 weeks. Remarkably, the remission rate was only 36.8% for this group of patients, who made at least one follow-up visit, with the mean time to response and also to remission being 6.3 weeks, and with over one-third of patients remitting after 9 weeks. But 16% of patients dropped out of this phase of the study due to "intolerance." Subsequently for those not responding adequately, Step 2 involved switching to one of three other antidepressants or cognitive therapy, or augmentation of citalopram with bupropion (Wellbutrin), buspirone (Buspar), or cognitive therapy. Step 3 involved any switch to mirtazepine or nortriptyline or augmentation with thyroid or lithium, while Step 4 involved switching to tranylcypromine (Parnate) or venlafaxine (Effexor) XR plus mirtazepine (Remeron). There was a cumulative remission rate of over 50% after two treatment steps, and almost 70% after four steps.

Data analysis of this rather representative sample of depressed STAR*D patients presents a realistic picture. Most depressions are treatment resistant, more so as the number of co-morbid psychiatric and co-morbid medical conditions increase. The shorter the time that the patient has been in a depressive episode, the more likely he or she will get a good outcome. Anxious patients take longer to respond and often have a less good response than those without prominent anxiety. For patients treated in an optimal fashion in the STAR*D trial, somewhat less than two-thirds will remit even after lengthy trials using switch or augmentation options. Those that just respond but do not remit are twice as likely to relapse. But the authors of the study point out that even though one-third of all patients enrolled in the study did not remit, even with multiple combinations of antidepressant treatments, still STAR*D did not evaluate all available treatments for depression. Whether it is true that more complex multiple drug regimens are burdensome, risky, or effective is an empirical question that deserves study.

An extremely important outcome point that should inform treatment practice from the STAR*D experience is that, of the ultimate responders, only two-thirds did so in six weeks, and of the ultimate remitters, only half did so by six weeks. What this means is that many clinicians probably have not been keeping their own patients on an antidepressant long enough at the highest tolerable dose before switching or augmenting.

TREATMENT-RESISTANT DEPRESSION

As seen from STAR*D, treatment-resistant depression (TRD), defined as failure to go into remission after several therapeutic trials at adequate dosage with good compliance and no active co-occurring substance abuse, is a very prevalent clinical problem.

There are a number of different strategies to employ when a compliant patient is not getting better: substituting (monotherapy), augmenting (polytherapy with psychiatric medications), or using adjunctive medications (those not commonly used by psychiatrists).

Substituting one drug for the next (switching) could be within class, such as the SSRIs like fluoxetine (Prozac), paroxetine (Paxil), citalopram (Celexa), and sertraline (Zoloft). Switching could also be going from one class of agents to another, such as using a serotonin and selective norepinephrine reuptake inhibitor (SNRI) like duloxetine (Cymbalta) or venlafaxine (Effexor), or using mirtazepine (Remeron) or bupropion (Wellbutrin). Not often used but still effective as monotherapy are the tricyclic antidepressants (TCAs) imipramine and amitriptyline plus nefazodone (with a recent black box warning because of rare but fatal hepatotoxicty) and the monoamine oxidase inhibitors (MAOIs) with their dietary and other medication restrictions (except for low-dose segeline).

Augmenting medications are added on to a well-tolerated and partially effective antidepressant to see if they will jump-start the healing process. Typically, mirtazepine or bupropion is added to an SSRI or venlafaxine. The second-generation antipsychotics also have some research data: For example, olanzapine (Zyprexa) added to fluoxetine showed good response in a limited number of patients with psychotic depressions; quetiapine (Seroquel) monotherapy in 300 mg showed promising results with some bipolar depressed patients; and risperidone (Risperdal), ziprasidone (Geodon), and aripiprazole (Abilify) show some promise. Aripiprazole has now been approved by the Food and Drug Administration (FDA) for adjunctive treatment for depression, starting at 2 to 5 mg/day and then uptitrated at weekly intervals to a target dose of 5 to 10 mg per day, with 15 mg the maximum recommended dose.

Sometimes a low dose of a tricyclic can be an effective augmentation agent. Other augmenting agents with some research support include buspirone (Buspar) and some of the psychostimulants: amphetamine/dextroamphetamine (Adderal) or methylphenidate (Ritalin). Lithium sometimes gives a gratifying response within a week, as does an adjunctive treatment, liothyronine (Cytomel). Adjunctive treatment with liothyronine (at 50 mcg) or levothyroxine at times can also provide a gratifyingly rapid and brisk response, again with low doses. Here the time frame is often one to two weeks.

What do the experts recommend for your patient? Augment if the patient is showing some response, but if there is none, switch. If the patient is anxious, augment with buspirone. Sleep problems, add mirtazepine. If the patient has anergia, loss of interest, or is lethargic, use bupropion. Aripiprazole has just received FDA approval for treatment-resistant depressions. These steps failing, use liothyronine first, then lithium. And always use hope. Plus exercise. Then think about using some of the novel augmenting medications.

None of the medications (except for olanzapine added to fluoxetine and aripiprazole) in Table 9.2 are FDA approved for use in supplementing antidepressants, so the patient should be told that these are

Table 9.2 Adjunctive and Augmenting Medications to Assist the
Effectiveness of Antidepressants

Lithium

Desipramine or nortriptyline

Dextroamphetamine mixed salts

Liothyronine or levothyroxine

Bupropion SR to be added to venlafaxine, SSRIs, or mirtazepine

Mirtazepine to be added to venlafaxine, SSRIs, or bupropion SR

Ziprasidone, quetiapine, aripiprazole, and olanzapine

Lamotrogine (FDA approved for bipolar but not major depression)

Buspirone (full agonist at presynaptic autoreceptor and partial agonist at
postsynaptic autoreceptor)

Pindolol (5-HT1A postsynaptic antagonist)

Pramipexole (Mirapex), a dopamine agonist used for Parkinson's disease and
restless leg syndrome

off-label usage. Similarly, using antidepressants as monotherapy in very high doses, which expert psychopharmacologists sometimes do, is off-label.

How long is long enough for an adequate drug trial? Experts advocate at least an eight-week drug trial. Of that span, at least four weeks, or even better six weeks, should be at the maximum tolerated dose before deciding that the medication is not working. Since some responders go on to remit after 12 weeks or more on a medication, it is best not to quit too soon, especially for the patient with multiple treatment failures. Of course, after a patient has been through several 12-week trials reaching the highest tolerable dose without going into remission, the chances are increasingly remote that remission will occur.

We say this not to discourage the clinician, but to encourage him or her to keep on trying to find the key that opens up the door to recovery. Hope is an important ingredient in the clinician's armamentarium. Almost all depressions remit in time if we can wait long enough. When additional improvement in a patient well known to you fails, it becomes important to not focus exclusively on symptomatology, which may paradoxically worsen a patient's psychological functioning and quality of life. Rather, it is important to use a disease management approach, focusing on how the patient can deal with his or her illness in the face of persistent symptoms. This approach works well in pain clinics as well as with diabetes, asthma, chronic fatigue syndrome, and arthritis.

But whenever a patient seems to be adherent to his or her medication regimen, is motivated to recover, and has failed to respond to numerous medication trials, one must always consider the possibility that the diagnosis is wrong. Perhaps the patient has a co-morbid substance problem that has not been addressed, a refractory pain problem, an insoluble and toxic psychosocial situation, or a medical co-morbidity such as subclinical hypothyroidism. Or perhaps the patient has a bipolar depression. A 2005 study by V. Sharma, M. Kahn, and A. Smith suggests that up to half of persons who have refractory depression actually have bipolar II disorder.

HOW LONG TO CONTINUE TAKING MEDICATION

Most patients don't want to take any medications for very long, especially adolescents and even patients up to middle age (but by that time, many people take so many medications, vitamins, and other supplements that taking one more tablet or capsule doesn't make much difference as long as there are no side effects). Taking medication is a recognition of one's vulnerability, and younger patients especially find that hard to face.

When the patient in remission is considering stopping his or her medication, it is important for the clinician to cite relevant research data to assist the patient's decision making. Reliable follow-up studies indicate that if a patient has had just one major episode of depression and goes off antidepressants, there is a 25 to 50% chance of another episode at some time. If there have been two episodes, the chances of a repeat are 75%; for three prior episodes, the likelihood is 90 to 95% for a recurrence. Moreover, the patient runs about an 11% risk each time a successful antidepressant is stopped that it won't be as effective the next time it is started. For the patient with a calamitous first episode, one might consider simply continuing on the antidepressant, since for most, depressions are recurrent.

NOVEL TREATMENTS

Neurostimulation therapies for depression, both acute and long term, are still in the early phase of development, including deep brain stimulation, vagal nerve stimulation, and repetitive magnetic brain stimulation. In addition to 6 to 12 sessions of unilateral or bilateral convulsive therapy, some patients do well on maintenance monthly or biweekly ECT treatments.

A few women with perimenopausal depression do well on estrogen replacement therapy, done in conjunction with the patient's gynecologist, to enhance the effectiveness of an SSRI. Estrogen may also reduce the response time and obviate the need to increase the antidepressant dosage.

Primapexole, which is a stage 5 treatment for the Texas logarithm for bipolar depression, has both neuroprotective and dopaminergic effects, with the potential for inducing compulsive behaviors (gambling) and perhaps other side effects. It has not been widely used yet in the field, but some effect sizes in small studies seem impressive. Again, like many newer treatments for depression, or even bipolar disorder, it is not FDA approved for treatment of depression.

PSYCHOEDUCATION

Psychoeducation is covered more fully in Chapter 5. David Burns, MD's, book *Feeling Good* has sold more than 3 million copies. It is an extraordinary paperback book that spells out in more than 600 pages the principles of cognitive behavioral therapy. A tale is told that half the patients in Stanford's Depression Clinic were given the book to read, and of those that got the book, half dropped off the waiting list as they had been able to treat their own depression adequately. At $8.00 to $16.50, it is truly a bargain. Patients should be encouraged only to read six pages or so the first time they look at the book, so that they won't be overwhelmed by the book's length.

There is also a self-help disease management workbook that can be downloaded, with information that is user-friendly, evidence based, and self-guided: www.comh.ca/resources > Antidepressant Skills Workbook.

Chapter 10

Working With the Bipolar Patient

The first point we wish to make in this quick-grab chapter is that there may be a one in four chance that the severely depressed patient sitting in front of you has an undetected, undiagnosed bipolar condition rather than a major unipolar depressive disorder. The average length of time that a bipolar patient spends in treatment with mental health professionals before being correctly diagnosed is ten years.

THE CHALLENGE OF MAKING THE DIAGNOSIS OF BIPOLAR DISORDER

Why? Patients rarely complain about energy spurts associated with euphoria, or even irritability. Such episodes may be unusual for the individual but not life shattering. And these episodes may have occurred decades ago. They usually are brief. Moreover, these patients generally don't complain about their roller coaster moods, unless prompted. They consider their impulsive shopping to be a character defect, and their increased libido or irritability to just happen, and not to be associated with an illness. Moreover, when patients are severely depressed, they see life through the lens' distortion of depression and have enough trouble recounting some aspects of depressed mood, let alone reflecting back on distant, sometimes far distant, episodes of hypomania, which do not seem to them, intuitively, to be related to the current depressed episode.

So, one must be proactive in ruling out hypomania, asking about recent or long distant roller coaster moods. Taking a thorough family history of diagnosed and undiagnosed suspect behavior plus getting a collaborative history from a partner or family members also helps to get a relevant and accurate personal and family history.

97

It is important with each depressed patient to go slowly through the *Diagnostic and Statistical Manual of Mental Disorders* (DSM-IV) criteria for hypomania, explaining that there may have been a few brief episodes even several decades ago of "energy spurts," as otherwise cursory questioning may not detect a cryptic bipolar disorder. This usually takes a few minutes, but can have huge implications for patient care.

The Mood Diagnostic Questionnaire, developed by Robert Hirschfeld, MD, is a widely used screening device. On one side of a sheet of paper, it takes about 60 seconds to have the patient answer the 13 questions in Table 10.1.

If the symptoms in Table 10.1 have caused moderate or severe problems, and the patient has scored seven or more positive responses, there is clinical reason to investigate further for the presence of bipolar disorder. Although the questionnaire cannot make a diagnosis, still

Table 10.1 Mood Disorders Questionnaire

Has there ever been a period of time when you were not your usual self and …

1. you felt so good or so hyper that other people thought you were not your normal self, or you were so hyper that you got into trouble?

2. you were so irritable that you shouted at people or started fights or arguments?

3. you felt much more self-confident than usual?

4. you got much less sleep than usual and found you didn't really miss it?

5. you were much more talkative or spoke much faster than usual?

6. thoughts raced through your head or you couldn't slow your mind down?

7. you were so easily distracted by things around you that you had trouble concentrating or staying on track?

8. you had much more energy than usual?

9. you were much more active or did many more things than usual?

10. you were much more social or outgoing than usual, for example, you telephoned friends in the middle of the night?

11. you were much more interested in sex than usual?

12. you did things that were unusual for you or that other people might have thought were excessive, foolish, or risky?

13. you spent money that got you or your family into trouble?

If you checked yes to more than one of the above, have several of these ever happened during the same period of time?

How much of a problem did any of these cause you—like being unable to work, having family, money, or legal troubles, or getting into arguments or fights?

the presence of seven or more positives, in a patient that says that these concurrent symptoms have caused significant distress, should alert the clinician to carefully try to *rule in* the diagnosis of bipolar, assuming the behaviors are observable and produce overall problems in living.

Is it important to give the patient the correct diagnosis? Absolutely. Antidepressants in a small portion of patients flip them into a major manic episode, or a mixed episode that may look like an agitated depression, perhaps with psychotic features. For other patients, the antidepressant may seem to be a quick fix, only to "poop out" in a few months. In such instances, the patient may then embark on more frequent episodes of depression and a roughening of the course of the illness. For the depressed patient with a previously undiagnosed bipolar condition, it is not unusual to hear that he or she has been on six or more antidepressant trials that have pooped out or been without success.

From taking a thorough history there may be clues to the presence of bipolar disorder (see Table 10.2). While none of these items are pathognomonic of bipolar disorder, the presence of one or several items gleaned from the history certainly can alert the clinician to this possibility of bipolar disorder.

Table 10.2 Items From History Taking That Point to Bipolar Rather Than Unipolar Depression

Symptoms When Depressed

Hypersomnia when depressed

Weight gains when depressed

Psychomotor retardation

Diurnal mood variation

Very severe affective symptoms or psychotic features

Less likelihood of self-reproach when depressed

Items From the History

Earlier age of onset (before age 21) than with unipolar depresssion

A prior history of postpartum depression

Considerable credit card debt for items often not needed or used very much

Roller coaster moods

Three or more marriages

Faster onset of depression in bipolar than unipolar depression

Family history of bipolar disorder, completed suicide, or multigenerational history of recurrent depressive or bipolar illness

THE IMPORTANCE OF PSYCHOEDUCATION

For most patients, the explanation of why they wake up some days profoundly depressed, isolative, and tearful, and other days normal or energetic, comes with a great sense of relief, since most of these mood fluctuations do not seem to be associated with changes in activities, external stressors, or attitudes of other family members. Many patients have an "Aha!" response when they discover they have bipolar illness. But others are more reserved and question the validity of the new diagnosis.

If the patient is not convinced that he or she has a bipolar condition, the likelihood that the patient will be adherent to appropriate medication management is small. Thus, for many reasons, it is useful to have Web sites and handout materials about the illness. (Psychoeducation is covered in Chapter 5.) Still, with some patients, it may be helpful *not* to rush to treatment, assuming the patient is not in great distress. Allowing the patient to become informed enough to buy into the diagnosis cements the treatment relationship.

There are a number of psychoeducational groups set up for families. Some clinics offer these because evidence has demonstrated improvement in the course of the patients' illness. Attending, then joining the Depressive Support Alliance, formerly the National Depressive Manic Depression Association, is another very important educational tool, as well, for many patients, as a very good support for the patient and his or her family. There are now chapters in most cities.

The use of professionally set up Web sites with vetted hyperlinks is also a good strategy. There is one through www.medem.com as a benefit of membership in the American Psychiatric Association. Having such a Web site now costs $350 per year. An example of such a basic Web site is www.guggenheim.yourmd.com. (See Chapter 6 about educational materials for patients and their families.)

NONPHARMACOLOGICAL TREATMENT

As with unipolar depressions, bipolar depressions benefit from psychotherapy (cognitive behavioral therapy (CBT), interpersonal, conflict resolution, and family-focused therapy). For the bipolar patient, the importance of routine in preventing recurrence is essential. Circadian stability means regular weekday *and* weekend times for going to bed and rising, meals and social contact, plus avoiding flights across multiple time zones. Ellen Frank, PhD, has compelling evidence that interpersonal therapy (ITP) can help stabilize personal disruptions, while social rhythm therapy can help prevent chronobiological disruptions. Singly or, even better, together, these strategies do improve the course of the illness.

Daily mood charting, for the patient with rapid or very rapid cycling, can be helpful for the patient as well as for the prescriber. The patient begins to better see the periodicity of the illness, which he or she can then strive to control. For the prescriber, it is easier to keep track of the interventions and their partial or more complete success.

Since a large percent of bipolar patients abuse alcohol or substances, it is important not only to stress sobriety but also to help the bipolar patient understand the deleterious impact on the course of his or her illness. Not infrequently, AA, NA, or CA plus chemical abuse treatment can help improve the outcome.

PHARMACOLOGICAL PRINCIPLES OF TREATING ACUTE EPISODES IN BIPOLAR PATIENTS

Basic to treatment of an acute episode is establishing the patient on a mood-stabilizing agent. Currently lithium, valproic acid (Depakote ER), or carbamazepine (Tegretol) are typically used for predominantly manic symptoms. Atypical antipsychotics are also sometimes used, often transiently. For bipolar depression, lamotrogine (Lamictal) in doses very gradually raised to 100–400 mg, or fluoxetine plus olanzapine (Sybyax) in doses of 6–12 mg and 25–50 mg, respectively, or quetiapine (Seroquel) in doses titrated up to 300–600 mg may be helpful. Sometimes one of the atypical antipsychotic agents is added to other types of mood-stabilizing agents if need be. Although monotherapy may be successful for the first five years of treatment, usually after that period of time, several mood-stabilizing agents end up being used together. In addition to an acute antidepressant effect, some of these agents may postpone for a while subsequent episodes of depression, or at least decrease their severity.

A very recent randomized placebo-controlled double-blind study of depressed bipolar patients not responding to mood stabilizers with or without an antidepressant demonstrated that modafinil (Provigil) in doses of 100 to 200 mg per day may improve (44%

response rate) depressive symptomatology. Rarely, electroconvulsive therapy (ECT) may become necessary if an episode of mania or depression becomes life threatening. During an acute depressive episode there may be a need for a benzodiazepine for agitation, and for a hypnotic, such as zolpidem (Ambien) or trazodone, for sleep.

Until very recently, it was controversial that antidepressants added to mood stabilizers might be helpful for depressed bipolar patients. True, some bipolar patients insist that a selective serotonin reuptake inhibitor (SSRI) has been helpful for their depressive episodes, and since there may be many different genetic types of bipolar, such patient claims may bear considering. However, a recent study demonstrated that bupropion or sertraline as an add-on to a mood-stabilizing agent had no benefit for the treatment of the bipolar disorder in 1,742 patients, compared to placebo. Moreover, there is now mounting evidence that antidepressants can be harmful to the course of illness in patients with bipolar illness. This certainly is the case when there is no mood stabilizer on board.

Although there has always been the concern that antidepressant agents may switch a depressed patient precipitously into mania, the more pressing issue is that antidepressant agents roughen the course of the illness. That is, the depressed bipolar patient may begin to rapid cycle, or have very rapid or ultra-rapid cycling, or even develop an agitated depression when taking an antidepressant. Rapid cycling has been noted in a third of patients enrolled in the large STEP-BD study. Proponents of the deleterious iatrogenic effect of antidepressants in bipolar illness point out that before antidepressants were used, rapid to ultra-rapid cycling in bipolar illness was rare.

Since many bipolar patients also have one or more severe concomitant anxiety disorders, it may be necessary to use an SSRI, but only after the patient has been on a mood-stabilizing agent. Currently, most clinicians tend to avoid using venlafaxine (Effexor) or duloxetine (Cymbalta) as the serotonin and selective norepinephrine reuptake inhibitors (SNRIs), and norepinephrine-blocking tricyclic antidepressants (TCAs), such as nortriptyline and desipramine, are regarded as more likely to flip the patient into mania than the other antidepressants. Typically many, but not all, co-morbid anxiety disorders tend to calm down when the affective disorder is under good control.

A major problem with using evidence-based treatment for maintenance of bipolar patients is that the data before STEP-BD were not based on large cohorts of patients, were largely limited to bipolar I patients, and excluded children, adolescents, and those with co-morbid psychiatric, substance abuse, or medical conditions. As always, treatment guidelines should not replace clinical judgment and individualized treatment plans.

PHARMACOLOGICAL ISSUES FOR MAINTENANCE

Although some bipolar patients do very well in between episodes, this certainly is not the case for many others, especially for those with bipolar II. The quality of life in between episodes is often seriously impacted by subsyndromal depressive features. The hallmark of good care for these patients is the development of a caring, informative, and available partnering relationship.

The two leading algorithms of bipolar illness are the Texas Implementation of Medication Algorithms, in which Trisha Suppes, MD, has played a lead role, and the Expert Consensus Guideline Series, in which Paul Keck, MD, had a lead role. Another algorithm is that developed by Gary S. Sachs, MD, with equipoise stratification in the STEP-BD program. The Food and Drug Administration (FDA) has approved the following for maintenance of bipolar: lithium, lamotrogine, olanzapine, and aripiprazole. Other drugs frequently used, though not FDA approved for maintenance, include divalproex, carbamazepine, oxcarbazepine, and other atypical antipsychotic agents.

NOVEL TREATMENTS

For refractory bipolar depression, augmentation with pramipexole (Mirapex), titrating up slowly from doses of 0.125 mg t.i.d. for the first week, has had some success. Thyroid supplement may be helpful, if subclinical hypothyroidism is suspected. Some even suggest ultra-high doses of thyroxin. For severe lethargy and fatigue during bipolar depression when patients are on mood stabilizers, consider 15 to 30 mg per day of methylphenidate and 100 to 200 mg of modafanil (Provigil).

Some of the other anticonvulsant medications that have also been used as mood stabilizers, but without a compelling database, include gabapentin (Neurontin), pregabalin (Lyrica), topiramate

(Topamax), and levetiracetam (Keppra). Oxcarbazepine (Trileptal) in doses of 1,200 to 2,400 mg has shown some promising results as a mood stabilizer. Nimodipine also has had some positive success. All of these agents are off-label.

Chapter II

Working With the Anxious Patient

In this quick-grab chapter, we discuss aspects of the interview with the very anxious patient and some of the challenges of treatment. If your patient has one anxiety disorder, do not be surprised to find several others.

DIAGNOSTIC ISSUES WITH GENERALIZED ANXIETY DISORDER

Patients with a generalized anxiety disorder usually present for the first time in the office as a fidgety, distressed, circumferential person that, often to the clinician's annoyance, talks rapidly in a nonstop manner under great pressure. Patients with anxiety symptoms usually show their discomfort. Still, since they have been trying to *avoid* feelings that augment their anxiety, they may try to avoid affirming that they have anxiety symptoms. Geriatricians working with elderly anxious patients have found that it is helpful to ask about their symptoms indirectly at first, for example: "How do you handle stressful situations? How often do these feelings occur? What do you do when this happens?"

When anxious people feel that they have permission to speak and ask questions, they often do so at great length, even asking the same question in many different ways, as if they have been too anxious to listen to the caregiver's response the first time. Clinicians should remember that the second and subsequent interviews with such patients are easier to bear, as the patient is reassured that he or she has survived the ordeal of the initial interview. The patient may no longer feel as urgent a need to control the interview—to lay out all the facts. The fear: "*What if* I left out some of the details, then the doctor couldn't understand my problem, so I couldn't be helped?"

With such a fearful, detail-oriented patient, sometimes it becomes necessary to impose polite but firm structure. If you need to interrupt the patient's overinclusive use of detail or pressured tangential speech, fear not. The patient has experienced redirection during many conversations before, and being courteous (rather than exasperated) will be much appreciated.

When a patient responds to the question "If there were an Olympic event for worriers, do you think you would win a gold medal?" with "gold" or "platinum," you've probably nailed the diagnosis, which, with a few other queries from *Diagnostic and Statistical Manual of Mental Disorders* (DSM-IV), will ensure the correct diagnosis of generalized anxiety disorder.

DIAGNOSTIC ISSUES WITH SOCIAL ANXIETY DISORDER

Although social anxiety disorder patients do not seem to present that frequently in the office for treatment, there are a lot of them out there. The National Comorbidity Survey Replication reports a lifetime prevalence of 12.1% and a 12-month prevalence of 7.1%.

Severe or disabling social anxiety occurs in multiple social situations, such as initiating a conversation, attending parties, dating, or participating in small group activities. Some patients are able to function very ably in professional situations, for example, functioning as a pastor in a large church, but experience severe social anxiety in the setting of real-life personal social activities not related to being the rector. Accompanying physical symptoms of social anxiety may include blushing, profuse sweating, palpitations, shaking, nausea, diarrhea, inability to urinate in a public rest room or to write in a public setting, and speech block. Behavioral symptoms include avoidance and "freezing up."

Often the diagnosis of social phobia is made when the patient presents for treatment of some other psychiatric condition. There is a lifetime co-morbidity of some other DSM-IV disorder in 63% to 90% of patients with social anxiety disorder. Many patients with social anxiety disorder self-medicate with alcohol, and excessive use is frequent.

When the patient responds positively to a question about sometimes avoiding social or even family gatherings if at all possible, a few follow-up questions, often read directly from DSM-IV, will usually lock in the diagnosis of social anxiety disorder.

DIAGNOSTIC AND ASSESSMENT ISSUES WITH OCD

Obsessive compulsive disorder (OCD) is a common anxiety disorder that, by contrast, is surprisingly not readily recognized. Before the correct diagnosis is made, the typical OCD patient will have sought treatment from three or four doctors and will have spent an average of nine years *in treatment*. The average time between the initial onset of symptoms and appropriate treatment is 17 years. These patients often think of their OCD symptoms as just part of their personality, or else they are ashamed of not being able to control their thoughts or behavior. When tactfully questioned, patients seen for obsessive compulsive disorder usually quickly affirm their habits of checking, their need for symmetry, their being a "neat freak," and their fear of contamination or their fear of acting out destructive sexual fantasies. But many patients seen for other psychiatric conditions, such as concomitant intermittent depressions, will often not spontaneously share their OCD symptoms with their psychiatrist, as they may have shame about having such ruminations.

> Reverend J was a beloved minister in his community. He had suffered from recurring depressions, some of which were severe, but none requiring hospitalization. He had been in treatment with a number of psychiatrists, but had never confided to any of them that he had sexual and violent fantasies that occupied much of his waking hours. Despite this handicap, he was able to counsel patients and deliver splendid sermons for decades.
>
> When his dose of sertraline (Zoloft) had to be raised to treat his depressive episode, he experienced, for the first time in three decades, some relief from his sexual and destructive obsessive thoughts. In this setting of unexpected OCD improvement, he was able to confess to his psychiatrist that he had long been having these secret obsessive thoughts.

Assessing the severity of OCD is facilitated by using the Yale-Brown OCD Scale (Y-BOCS), a self-report scale, which should be administered at the start of treatment and then at least every six months, to measure the patient's progress: *recovery* (Y-BOCS of 8 or less), *remission* (Y-BOCS of 16 or less), or having a treatment *response*

(Y-BOCS score reduced by 25 to 35%). The Y-BOCS Symptom Check List provides information about problem areas for further follow-up.

Diagnostic issues may arise when the patient has poor insight into his or her obsessions, which can be difficult to distinguish from a delusion. Diagnoses of patients that may show OCD traits but not be diagnosed with OCD include body dysmorphic disorder, with obsessions about defect in body image; hypochondriasis, with preoccupation about the likelihood of serious medical disease(s); and anorexia nervosa, consumed with fears just about weight and fatness. Finally, those patients with pervasive development disorders of childhood (autism, Asperger's) often have stereotyped or repetitive motor mannerisms but should not be diagnosed as OCD.

DIAGNOSING AND ASSESSING OTHER ANXIETY DISORDERS

Emergency room physicians or hospitalists are often the first to make the diagnosis of a panic disorder. Regrettably, many patients are sent home with the offhand comment: "There's nothing wrong with you; it's all in your head!" When the patient does come to the mental health clinician's office, he or she readily affirms the presence of panic or anxiety attacks. A quick run through the 13 criteria for panic disorder (just 4 are needed) of the multiple somatic symptoms listed in DSM-IV reaffirms diagnosis.

In similar fashion, patients that suffer from specific phobias generally don't present with diffuse answers and pressured responses to questions. They typically know what the problem is: They can't cross a bridge or they can't fly in an airplane.

Patients with posttraumatic stress disorder (PTSD) can readily relate the onset of their symptoms to a specific traumatic event. That trauma may have been recent or remote, but the flashbacks and distressing dreams are usually quite specific. The PTSD patient can also readily tie in symptoms of hypervigilance and exaggerated startle to PTSD. Such patients, however, often do not relate symptoms of abulia, the inability to get off the sofa, the diminished interest or participation in significant events, and the feelings of estrangement to their PTSD. Nor do PTSD patients necessarily relate symptoms of irritability or outbursts of anger and the difficulty with concentration to the diagnosis of PTSD.

ATTEMPTS AT SELF-HELP AND INITIATING MEDICATION MANAGEMENT

Many patients with anxiety disorders, in their own desperate attempts at self-help, have resorted to alcohol in excessive amounts, over-the-counter sedative hypnotics as sleep aids, or even street drugs. They may also have used family members' benzodiazepines, for example, lorazepam (Ativan), alprazolam (Xanax), clonazepam (Klonopin), and so forth. It is best to proactively ferret out this information and then develop whatever potentially lengthy tapering off, or prescribed maintenance, as seems appropriate.

Still, when anxious patients receive a prescription, even though they have been heavily self-medicating with unknown street drugs, they still may prove to be initially reluctant to start prescription medication. So used to obsessing about "What if?" questions, they become terribly frightened about potential prescribed medication side effects. Even when they do start to take their medication, after much initial reassurance and a considerable delay in the start date, they usually will continue to scan themselves for any possible side effect. Upon finding even a minimal one, they are likely to consider that they are having a toxic or potentially incapacitating outcome, believing the worst. Reassurance that the side effects they are experiencing are common and transient usually helps. But starting with a very low dose of medication and slowly titrating up to a therapeutic level will save much angst.

CAFFEINE, THE UNSUSPECTED VILLAIN

Most Americans drink caffeinated beverages, including coffee, iced tea, and cola drinks. Few think about the fact that ingesting more than 250 mg caffeine daily can result in symptoms of anxiety, tremors, and sleep problems. Although caffeinism is only rarely the sole cause of an anxiety disorder, it is essential to quantitate caffeine intake. When the patient says that he or she drinks two cups of coffee per day, it is imperative to determine the size of the cup, since Dunkin Donuts and other national brands do have 32-ounce cups of hot or iced coffee. Tea is another source of caffeine, as is Mountain Dew. Some cola drinks contain 75 mg of caffeine or more. There are also now some caffeinated "sports drinks." Tapering off a substantial caffeine habit may take one or several months of gradual withdrawal. The peril

Table 11.1 Amount of Caffeine in Drinks

Starbucks coffee grande, 16 oz	330 mg
Monster, 16 oz	160 mg
Rockstar, 16 m	160 mg
Starbucks caffe latte, 16 oz	150 mg
Jetset, 10.5 oz	120 mg
Plain brewed coffee, 8 oz	95mg
Red Bull, 8.3 oz	76 mg
Esspresso, 1 oz	64 mg
Black tea, brewed, 8 oz	47 mg
Coca Cola Classic, 12 oz	35 mg
Green tea, brewed, 8 oz	30–50 mg
Snapple ice tea, 16 oz	18 mg
Decaffeinated brewed coffee, 8 oz	2 mg

Source: Data compiled and adapted from http://www.
mayoclinic.com/health/caffeine/AN01211

of a too rapid pace of caffeine withdrawal is the precipitation of severe pounding headaches. The consumer-friendly and reliable Mayo Clinic Web site lists caffeine in various drinks (Table 11.1).

In making the diagnosis of an anxiety disorder, a family history is usually informative for someone being "neurotic" or "nervous." A bonus: If the patient knows a medication that helped a blood relative, it may also be useful for him or her.

A family history of alcoholism or substance abuse is particularly helpful in the management of patients with anxiety disorders, for that means that the patient may require higher than usual doses of benzodiazepam medications and is at an increased risk of rapidly developing physiological dependence. Although only about half of patients with a history of alcoholism abuse their prescribed benzodiazepines, it is hard to predict which half your patient will belong to. Developing drug dependency in your patient is too high a risk to take, so it is best not to go down this route with an anxious patient with a family history of substance/alcohol dependency or abuse.

PHARMACOLOGICAL TREATMENT ISSUES WITH THE ANXIETY DISORDERS

Although pharmaceutical industry-sponsored data routinely showcase the efficacy of selective serotonin reuptake inhibitors (SSRIs) and serotonin and selective norepinephrine reuptake inhibitors (SNRIs) in comparison to placebos in randomized controlled double-blind clinical trials with patients with anxiety disorders, clinicians need to be prepared that a substantial number of their patients will not respond as favorably. Of note, those that do respond may need to have higher dosages and for lengthier periods of time than for patients with depression before they respond. When starting a patient on an antidepressant, it becomes important to start at a lower than usual dosage, for example, 25 mg of sertraline (Zoloft), 10 mg of citalopram (Celexa), 37.5 mg of venlafaxine (Effexor XR), to minimize the initial exacerbation of anxiety or panic. Many of the medications for anxiety described below are "off label" (non-FDA approved for anxiety disorder, although approved for other disorders).

Thus, benzodiazepines, diazepam (Valium), lorazepam (Ativan), alprazolam (Xanax), and so forth, plus buspirone (Buspar), gabapentin (Neurontin), and pregabalin (Lyrica) all may have their place in the treatment of generalized anxiety disorder. Because of the slow onset of the SSRIs and SNRIs, it is often helpful temporarily to pre-scribe a long-acting benzodiazepine such as clonazepam (Klonopin) or other psychotropic agent to partially cover the anxiety until the longer-term, better-solution antidepressant starts to work. However, benzodiazepines should probably be avoided if the patient has a prior history of substance abuse or a strong family history of addictions.

As mentioned, the main adverse effect of the benzodiazepines is physiological dependency and occasional addiction. The main side effect of the benzodiazepines is sedation. In the middle aged, especially over age 65, unsteadiness of gait may be a problem. The elderly can become quite forgetful or even confused. Some patients come to treatment already abusing benzodiazepines, and their physical dependence requires some detoxification. Even after pro-longed regular use, there may need to be a very lengthy taper. New evidence suggests that the benzodiazepines may actually undercut the learning processes of cognitive behavioral therapy (CBT).

Other agents have been used for generalized anxiety and other anxiety disorders. Buspirone has shown some utility. Buspirone is an anti-anxiety drug that is not abused, but it does take up to three weeks to become effective, and it is only effective for about half of the anxious patients that take it.

The atypical antipsychotic agents have shown efficacy as aug-menting antidepressants in randomized controlled clinical trials, but there are concerns about the development of extrapyramidal symptoms, tardive dyskinesia, weight gain, and the metabolic syndrome. The antiepileptic agents gabapentin and pregabalin in rather high doses have also had some success in a few reports.

For patients with social anxiety, remission refers to the elimination of pathological levels of avoidance and fear, although there still may be some anxiety in social settings, which is part of everyday living. Treatment can provide a significant improvement in quality of life. The typical treatment plan could consist of an SSRI titrated to a high dose for many months plus CBT focusing on gradually facing what had been avoided. The patient's prior habit of avoidance did lead to a temporary reduction in fear, but that only reinforced avoidant behavior. After successful response to medication, discontinuation after only 12 weeks can lead to high relapse rates, while discontinuation after 5 to 12 months after relief of symptoms leads to lower relapse rates of 20 to 60% over the next six months.

For social anxiety, some non-SSRI medications that have been shown to be effective include mirtazepine (Remeron), gabapentin (Neurontin), and pregabalin (Lyrica). Quetiapine (Seroquel) and olanzapine (Zyprexa) have each shown signs of efficacy in small controlled trials but require further study.

For patients with specific (rather than generalized) social anxiety disorders, such as giving public talks, propranolol (Inderal) has demonstrated efficacy in nervous performers. Even some medical residents, compelled to present at grand rounds, say that they have benefited from taking a single dose of 20 mg of propranolol one hour before the anticipated situation. The peripherally acting, nonlipophilic beta-blocker atenolol (Tenormin) has no direct central nervous effects on anxiety, but it does diminish tremor and palpitations. For musicians, for example, taking a single dose of 25 mg of atenolol prior to a performance can be very reassuring in stressful situations, since the presence of tremor signals to them that they have increased anxiety, starting a vicious cycle. Beta-blockers, however, are of little value in generalized social anxiety disorder.

For patients with OCD, the SSRIs are all about equally effective, with fluvoxamine (Luvox) frequently chosen. Those patients that fail to respond to one serotonin reuptake inhibitor (SRI) may well respond to another SRI. OCD tends to require higher doses of SRIs than those used to treat depression. The tricyclic clomipramine (Anafranil) is also a good medication for this illness. The typical target dose for clomipramine is 250 mg, also the maximum dose. For fluvoxamine, the target dose is 200 mg and the maximum is 300 mg. For sertraline the target dose is 150 mg and the maximum is 225 mg. Meta-analyses suggest that clomipramine may be superior to other SRIs.

Initial response to treatment for the OCD patient is usually more delayed than the response seen in depression, and may take 8 to 12 weeks. Atypical antipsychotics are the only proven augmenting agents in SRI nonresponders. In responders, SRIs should be continued for a minimum of one to two years, and perhaps lifelong in those patients with persistent symptoms and for those with multiple relapses.

For patients with PTSD, pharmacotherapy with an SSRI such as sertraline may be a good initial choice. Results of treatment when this disorder has become chronic are often less than desired, leading to the frequent use of augmentation with atypical antipsychotics.

For the disabling nightmares, the Veterans Affairs (VA) experience with combat veterans indicates that the antihypertensive agent prazocin (Minipres) can be very helpful, with doses gradually titrated up over a month to 10 to 15 mg at night, starting out at 1 mg to avoid the "first-night hypotension" of this alpha-1 adrenergic antagonist.

For those patients with anxiety disorders that have received a partial remission, psychotherapy strategies of relaxation, meditation, or more formal CBT may be helpful to target residual anxiety and reduce the risk of recurrence.

PSYCHOLOGICAL TREATMENT OF THE ANXIETY DISORDERS

Patient preference, severity of the disorder, and the availability of a therapist skilled in doing CBT are some of the determinants of whether patients will have pharmacotherapy, pharmacotherapy with CBT, or CBT alone. Some patients do not want or have the patience or do not have the inclination to undertake CBT. Others will be so medication phobic that they will not want any somatic treatment, which is a good segue to introducing the concept of CBT. In mild to moderate anxiety disorders, specifically tailored CBT can be very effective for generalized anxiety, social phobia, panic disorder, PTSD, and OCD.

Research data, reviews, and meta-analyses from 2003 to 2006 for generalized anxiety disorder do not indicate that there is an added benefit of combined treatment over stand-alone treatment. Some studies do demonstrate a quicker initial response to medication. Studies of CBT with follow-up over one to two years favor CBT. *Overcoming Anxiety for Dummies,* by L. L. Smith and C. H. Elliott, has been well received by patients as a self-help book.

CBT for social anxiety combines psychoeducation, teaching of cognitive restructuring skills, and practice: first with imagined social situations, then with exposure to feared social situations with role playing and homework assignments. But first the patient must be assessed to make certain that he or she has actually acquired adequate social skills, and just fails to use them in a feared social setting. For patients that do lack basic social competency, systematic training in social skills is a necessity. Later exposure to those feared situations is followed by debriefing and further role playing. When CBT was compared to fluoxetine (Prozac) at one year's follow-up, CBT remained superior to fluoxetine plus self-exposure, and self-exposure with placebo. Combining CBT and pharmacotherapy did yield the most rapid effects.

CBT for OCD patients often centers on exposure and response prevention. Relapse rates for OCD patients appear to be greater for those just treated with medications than for those just treated with CBT. After five years of treatment, about half of OCD patients no longer meet criteria for OCD. CBT is an effective treatment modality. It should be considered for all OCD patients, and is a potential option in SRI nonresponders.

For PTSD patients, new research has demonstrated that early treatment with cognitive therapies may sometimes actually prevent PTSD from emerging. When started within a month after the trauma, CBT using prolonged exposure showed efficacy at four months, whereas citalopram (Celexa) at 20 mg did not, nor did a placebo. This positive outcome for CBT may have impacted the acquisition phase of the disorder before the disorder became more chronic.

THE BENEFITS OF EITHER COMBINED SOMATIC AND PSYCHOLOGICAL TREATMENT OR MONOTHERAPY

For patients with anxiety disorders, initial combined treatment followed by the choice of one or the other modality would seem to be a reasonable option. For example, with a patient with a devastating series of panic attacks that have sent him or her to the ER, the use of *sublingual* generic alprazolam, with strict weekly limits, might help to jump-start whatever type of therapy is eventually chosen.

For panic disorder, either pharmacological or CBT treatments alone have demonstrated greater cost-efficacy over combined treatment, with imipramine representing the most cost-effective treatment option at the completion of the acute phase, and CBT representing the most cost-efficacious option at the end of maintenance treatment and six months after treatment termination. CBT emerges, based on current reviews, as the most durable and cost-effective monotherapy.

For OCD, CBT alone with exposure *in vivo* and response prevention, sometimes coupled with fluvoxamine (Luvox) or clomipramine (Anafranil), is usually quite effective. Combined treatment for OCD has the added benefit of considerable improvement in mood, if that is a problem.

PTSD patients treated with sertraline and prolonged exposure therapy tend to maintain their clinical improvement more than those just treated with sertraline alone. Treatment for severe PTSD is far from satisfactory, whatever modalities are selected. SSRIs and atypical antipsychotic agents do help somewhat to take the edge off.

NOVEL TREATMENTS

Treatment for almost half of patients with anxiety disorders has far from satisfactory outcomes. Although there are few rigorously conducted trials of the antiepileptic drugs in the treatment of anxiety disorders, gabapentin and more recently pregabalin in higher doses have had some favorable reports, as have divalproexic (Depakote ER) and now levetiracetam (Keppra). None of these novel treatments have been FDA approved for the treatment of anxiety disorders, but they have been approved for the treatment of other conditions.

Topiramate (Topamax), often used by psychiatrists to help prevent weight gain in patients on Zyprexa (olanzapine), Seroquel (quetiapine), or lithium, can reduce sweating in patients with social anxiety disorder that are profoundly embarrassed by their sweating. The antihypertensive agent terazosin (Hytrin) is sometimes successful in decreasing distressing sweating.

Preventive propranolol treatment for PTSD, with accident victims started on this medication while still in the emergency room, seems to be showing some promise in a few studies.

What is on the horizon? The use of D-cycloserine (Seromycin), a partial agonist at the N-methyl-D-aspartate receptor, in combination with CBT, may hold some promise. This agent has been shown to improve fear behavior in rodents and in some patients with acrophobia or social phobia during exposure-based CBT.

For OCD, ablative neurosurgical approaches have been used sometimes for the most severely afflicted, unresponsive to many maximum treatment modalities. Anterior capsulotomy, limbic leucotomy, and cingulotomy are all non-FDA approved. Deep brain stimulation is currently undergoing experimental work in several centers. This procedure is only minimally invasive; its effects are reversible.

Chapter 12

Working With the Traumatized Patient

In this quick-grab chapter, we discuss some of the psychological and pharmacological interventions with victims of such traumas as rape, severe motor vehicle accidents, severe burns, or fire fights/combat in military or civilian settings. An estimated 8 to 10% of the U.S. population experiences posttraumatic stress disorder (PTSD) at some point in their lives. The type of trauma dictates the likelihood of developing PTSD. For motor vehicle accidents, the incidence is 10%, while for rape it is 60%. Risk factors for developing PTSD include severity of trauma, continued exposure to stress and trauma, history of abuse and neglect, genetic predisposition to affective or other disorders, and limited social support. Resiliency is shown in those with self-sufficiency, optimism, cognitive ability and flexibility, faith and spirituality, and a resiliency gene.

A typical response to a traumatic incident is to be very shaken up, upset, crying, angry, anxious. Some patients instead may be numb or even have some dissociative symptoms. It is quite unusual for a mental health worker to see someone in his or her office within two days to four weeks of a traumatic event (the time limits for duration of an acute stress disorder), since during this time patients are usually seeing their primary care physician (PCP), clergy, and family. Only when symptoms continue and cause considerable distress and interfere with functioning is the mental health professional usually consulted. Therefore, most of us have little occasion to see patients acutely after exposure to an event that involved actual or threatened death or serious injury, with the patient's response being intense fear, helplessness, or horror.

By the time a patient is seen in the office following a trauma, usually after a month or so, the diagnosis of posttraumatic stress disorder is made based on:

117

1. Behavioral avoidance of anything that would arouse recollections of the trauma (thoughts, feelings, conversations, activities, places, people)
2. An increased nervous system arousal, marked by difficulty sleeping, irritability, restlessness, increased vigilance, exaggerated startle response, and difficulty concentrating
3. Persistently reexperiencing the event with recurrent images, thoughts, dreams, flashback episodes, or a sense of reliving the experience (flashbacks)
4. Dissociative symptoms, such as:

   Subjective sense of numbing, detachment, or absence of emotional responsiveness
   Reduction in awareness of the surroundings (being dazed)
   Derealization
   Depersonalization
   Dissociative amnesia

PHARMACOTHERAPY

There is little that is new for the management of chronic PTSD. Two selective serotonin reuptake inhibitors (SSRIs) have been approved for its treatment, sertraline (Zoloft) and fluoxetine (Prozac). These agents may help somewhat, but one should not expect remission, just some improvement. At times, the severity of the symptomatology, without much relief from an SSRI, may call for the off-label use of an atypical antipsychotic agent, for example, risperidone (Risperdal) and ziprasidone (Geodon). One should avoid prescribing benzodiazepines such as lorazepam (Ativan), alprazolam (Xanax), or clonazepam (Klonopin), as dose escalation often occurs in patients frantic to get relief. Moreover, there is a very high co-morbidity with substance dependence or abuse.

There are, however, new pharmacological treatments for the acute treatment of potentially *impending* PTSD and for relief of some PTSD symptoms.

There is a growing though still tentative research database that PTSD may be prevented in the patient with acute stress disorder, or even the person judged likely to develop such a syndrome in the early hours after a trauma. Intervention is with propranolol (Inderal), 80 to 120 mg per day for 10 days. Obviously, there may be problems giving a beta-blocker to an asthmatic. This simple technique, commenced in the emergency room within six hours of the trauma to patients with a resting pulse rate of over 80 beats per minute, seems to be associated with the prevention of the development of terror responses associated with the recollection of the traumatic event. Other studies, however, have not yet confirmed these results.

Nightmares are one of the most disturbing of all the symptoms associated with a traumatic event. Recently, the use of an off-label medication, the alpha-1 blocker prazocin (Minipress), an antihypertensive agent also used in benign prostatic hypertrophy, has found a role in extinguishing posttraumatic nightmares. Since prazocin is an antihypertensive agent, the prescriber needs to be aware of the possibility of orthostatic or other hypotension. But the doses used to extinguish nightmares, with a gradual escalation from 1 to 13 mg, are not considered to be antihypertensive doses.

Insomnia can sometimes be treated successfully with the off-label antidepressant trazodone, in doses of 50 to 200 mg. Priapism is rarely a worry at low doses.

One of the most reliable treatments for PTSD is "tincture of time." That is, PTSD symptoms usually subside gradually over time. One large-scale study has identified seven years as the mean time for PTSD symptoms to extinguish. However, if another traumatic event occurs, or if the individual retires and is no longer as busy as before, some or all of the PTSD symptoms can reemerge.

NOVEL PHARMACOLOGICAL TREATMENTS

Intravenous hydrocortisone, to reduce the hypothalamic-pituitary (HPA) axis activation, acting as a countermeasure to elevated corticotrophin-releasing factor, has been shown in a few patients to reduce the development of PTSD. Opioids to inhibit the HPA axis are another area under investigation. Benzodiazepines have been found to be unhelpful, and perhaps harmful in patients with acute trauma.

Imipramine, in a seven-day randomized double-blind trial, compared to chloral hydrate in pediatric burn patients, decreased the acute stress disorder symptoms significantly.

Neuropeptide Y agonists, substance P antagonists, and CRH antagonists are thought to have some promise.

PSYCHOLOGICAL TREATMENT

Acute stress disorder symptoms resemble those of PTSD, so the hope is that PTSD could be prevented with some type of psychological intervention. In the last two decades, critical incident debriefing (CID) had become the vogue. But current research now indicates that, at least for some patients, this procedure may actually be quite harmful. For the calm and collected patient without symptoms of an acute stress disorder, if it is necessary for forensic purposes to gather data, CID seems to carry no risk. But for the highly agitated patient, recounting *and reliving* the trauma actually tends to produce more PTSD symptoms later on, according to recent well-conducted research.

Recollecting is one thing, but brief one-time reliving the situation should be avoided. By contrast, when a patient has chronic PTSD, with pathological responses coming on as an established conditioned reflex, research data over the past decade have demonstrated that prolonged exposure to the sights and sounds of the event, reliving it, has become an established technique that gradually seems to diminish the conditioned reflex. There is now significant literature on a variety of prolonged exposure therapies.

Chapter 13

Working With the Angry or Violent Patient

In this quick-grab chapter, we focus on that patient most likely to get the mental health workers irritated or upset: the angry patient. We focus on diagnostic and management issues encountered when working with a patient that has been very angry in the recent or remote past. (Safety issues for the clinician with the violence-prone patient are addressed in Chapter 26.) To know one angry patient is to know one angry patient: It is very hard to generalize about a given individual, since anger is part of many different psychiatric Axis I and Axis II diagnoses. But there are some useful basic approaches to consider. Of course, not all anger is pathological. Some events, if correctly understood, would make anyone angry. But recurrent rage attacks merit attention.

THE ASSERTIVENESS CONTINUUM

Some anger is misperceived, when it actually is still far to the left, as part of the assertiveness–hostility–aggression continuum. The patient's assertiveness, actually not escalating hostility, may be incorrectly recognized due to the patient's learned familial traditions or ethnic tradition of expression. Still, the clinician can almost always tell when anger is really over the top.

Some anger is episodic, the lingering aftermath of severe brain injury associated with coma from meningitis or closed head injury. These people experience a very "shortened fuse," an irritability that is annoying to both patient and those around him or her. This may be the only remnant that is clinically apparent from the distant brain injury. Patients sometimes can learn, with motivation, and sometimes can be helped by medication, to control their outbursts much of the time.

INTERMITTENT EXPLOSIVE DISORDER

Some anger rises to the level of a psychiatric diagnosis such as intermittent explosive disorder (IED), where the clinical features are the inability (or unwillingness) to refrain from acting on the impulse to be very destructive, and acting out of proportion to the instigating event. Although head trauma in such patients is not uncommon, sometimes it is hard to ferret out if the head trauma might be the cause, or the effect, of the disorder. Often, however, there is no such known history of head trauma. How many IED attacks per year are needed to meet criteria? The current thinking of clinical experts in this area is that about three such episodes per year usually merits a diagnosis of IED. The prevalence of the disorder varies between 5.4% and 7.3% of the adult population, depending upon how IED is defined.

Patients with this disorder are almost always calm and peaceful in the office and rarely display irritability toward the clinician. Sometimes they appear to be bewildered and not very psychologically minded about the incident. It is not unusual for such patients to show up subdued, straightforward, and puzzled, asking for help to stop the inappropriate angry outbursts. Often a spouse or worried significant other will accompany the patient to a first office visit.

With IED, the anger seems to come on in an unexpected and unpremeditated moment, often in the setting of domestic quarrels, or perhaps at a social gathering, bar room, or sports game. Patients seen in a private practice setting are usually emphatic that it is property, not people, that is the target of their rage: walls, doors, windows, furniture, or kitchen utensils. Remorse is often expressed, and not just for the inconvenience it has caused the patient. It is unclear if persons seen with rage attacks in a prison setting will have different prodromes, targets, and feelings after their rage attacks.

In addition to cognitive behavioral therapy for IED, off-label therapeutic trials of medication appear to be indicated. The anticonvulsant divalproexic (Depakote ER) has some success in small case studies. Anecdotal data support oxcarbazepine (Trileptal) as having some benefit. There are also data that the selective serotonin reuptake inhibitor (SSRI) fluoxetine may be helpful.

ANXIETY AND OTHER SOURCES
UNDERPINNING THE ANGER

Underlying many of the angry episodes that patients experience is the anxiety of being threatened. The anxiety in some may merely last microseconds before the anger bursts forth. Sometimes the perceived threat may be considerably magnified if, for example, the patient has a paranoid personality disorder, a depressive disorder with a persecutory delusion, or an unmedicated or undermedicated actively psychotic schizophrenic disorder.

Anger is also often described in patients classified as having a Type A personality in the literature on coronary artery disease. Angry outbursts are also characteristic of attention-deficit hyperactivity disorder (ADHD) patients. Unmitigated rage also sometimes pours forth when a person with a narcissistic personality disorder suffers a severe blow to his or her (not so apparent) fragile self-esteem. Patients with conduct disorders or antisocial personality disorders may not be concerned about the carnage they cause, unless after the fact they feel an urge to show contrition to mitigate possible punishment.

Irritability sometimes gives way to anger and rage. Patients with grandiosity from Axis I conditions also can pour forth irritability that may morph into anger if upset in their endeavors. Some manic patients come across to their families as short-tempered with minimal stress. There may be elements of grandiose entitlement, perhaps just a short fuse as with an inability to tolerate any frustration, whether it be a personal interaction or even loud noise. When patients are actively psychotic and unmedicated, it may be difficult for the clinician to understand just what might unintentionally "push the button" to unleash a rageful and unpremeditated spontaneous assault.

An important aspect of treatment of Axis I disorders with anger comes from data in the recent CATIE study of 1,410 patients with chronic schizophrenia. Findings are that 19% of these patients were involved in violent behavior within the past six months, with 3.6% of the total group having a history of serious violent behavior. Being unmedicated or undermedicated for the actively psychotic patient with schizophrenia can lead to tragedy (see Chapter 26).

SUBSTANCE USE

Intoxicated patients or those withdrawing from substances that they have been addicted to represent other types of patients liable to rage attacks. They manifest an inability to control the urge to become aggressive when challenged. They may manifest their rage toward the clinician, or others, without any hint of social inhibition.

"Saturday night specials" and late-night boisterous drunks populate urban ERs and police lockups. However, some previously violent patients do at times come of their own volition to the clinician's office. Here a good sense of smell of whiskey may alert the clinician to the etiology of the patient's irritable and erratic behavior. Doing any therapeutic work with an inebriated patient is not conducive to any therapeutic progress and indicates a need for the clinician to demonstrate limit setting. Indeed, inebriation in the office may be an indication that the patient first needs to control substance abuse before further mental health treatment can continue. Of course, concurrent treatment is certainly preferable, but that may not be possible in all cases.

A rare slip into a brief episode of substance use, without consequences to the patient or others, may merely indicate an area of psychological vulnerability that later needs to be explored in a gentle fashion. But sometimes the patient's appearing intoxicated in the clinician's office indicates that the patient's therapy has not really been helpful, since the hidden substance problem may lie behind the mental health issues discussed in treatment. No creative outcome can occur from doing psychotherapeutic work with an intoxicated patient.

My personal experience with violent patients comes from work as a medical resident in a charity hospital's medical ward, in academic, state, and Veterans Affairs (VA) hospitals, and in a community mental health center (but never in any correctional setting or on any forensic units). In my practice, I have seen manic patients injure six staff attendants at a time when psychotic, men convicted of murder in the past engage in heated battle on a medical ward, and intermittently violent patients. I have found that these same individuals, who committed heinous acts in a fit of passion or psychotic rage in the past, yet in a calm setting without symptomatic mental illness, can be as sensitive and empathic as nonviolent patients. It would seem that the clinician, in a safe setting with a good therapeutic relationship established with a nonpsychotic patient, can gently probe into what was so threatening to the patient when he or she felt a need to protect his or her interests with an angry outburst.

THE UNSEEN SIDE OF VIOLENCE

A surprising new finding is that more people have anger attacks than panic attacks. This is a finding from the very recent National Comorbidity Survey Replication, based on household surveys of more than 9,000 U.S. adults, according to Ron Kessler, PhD, the dean of psychiatric epidemiologists. People with depression or panic attacks often seek professional help for such problems, but they generally do not do so for their rage fits. Moreover, when we interview our patients, we only rarely ask them routinely if they have rage attacks, although that information certainly can come out in the taking of a good history in a relaxed setting.

WHEN YOU MAY NOT WANT TO KNOW TOO MUCH

We routinely ask our patients at intake if they are currently having suicidal or homicidal ideation. But the reasons that we don't routinely ask about a past history of violence has not been well studied. One can speculate that our hesitation to ask about this behavior is that too much knowledge can lead to consequences outside the scope of the main reason the patient presented for help. For example, we don't routinely ask depressed mothers if they have been guilty of child abuse now or in the past. If the clinical history leads to a clear conclusion that children are at risk, obviously it must be dealt with according to the laws of the state. Of course, we always do ask depressed mothers the less challenging and more open-ended question about how the children in the family are faring. If the patient wishes to confess something, it is our obligation to help them deal with the issues.

Another example of how specific knowledge or its absence can be problematic follows:

> Mr. K is a 53-year-old divorced athletic man on SSDI that presented for treatment of depression associated with bipolar II. Although he has a gruff demeanor, he is quite a friendly and spirited philosopher with considerable self-obtained erudition, gained during his 10-plus years in a state prison. He is clearly working hard to be adherent to his complex medication regimen and has improved considerably, now only being mildly dysthymic.
>
> As his ability to concentrate and his energy level improved, it became important to formulate a plan of recovery that included increasing his level of participation in outside activities. When the patient was casually queried about part-time work he had done in the past, he off-handedly volunteered that he was an "enforcer" for some of his (probably mafia) friends.

Detailed knowledge and charting of certain information can present ethical, moral, practical, and therapeutic dilemmas often resolved by "not going there" unless the patient indicates that he or she wants to work on some feelings (of guilt) about an assault issue.

Dealing with highly charged issues, especially when they come up in the middle of the 20-minute hour, requires a quick reappointment. Some clinicians keep "secret holes" in their schedule each day or each week so they can have extra time to deal with totally unexpected emerging hot clinical issues.

Chapter 14

Working With the Somatizing Patient

In this quick-grab chapter, we focus on getting some satisfaction in working with a type of patients that many primary care physicians (PCPs) hate to care for, patients that are not rare in their practices, especially since these patients make so many visits. It is rare for somatizing patients to go for a year without seeing a physician, and not unusual for them to have multiple, urgent unscheduled requests to be seen by their PCP each quarter, typically for complaints that do not merit a clear-cut medical diagnosis.

SOMATIZATION DISORDERS

The prevailing wisdom is that patients with somatization disorder are usually better seen in a primary care setting than in a mental health specialty setting. Many somatizing patients, already feeling misunderstood and disrespected, feel even further put down when referred out to a mental health specialist and fail to keep their initial referrals.

G. Richard Smith, MD, and Roberta Monson, MD, more than two decades ago demonstrated that when internists were coached on how to manage their somatizing patients, their patients got much better outcomes on a variety of parameters. What advice did they follow? First, see these somatizing patients briefly but on a regular and frequent basis, rather than emulating usual care in the community (with infrequent but then urgent unscheduled appointments). When these patients are seen much less frequently, their urgent somatic complaints often elicit unnecessary diagnostic interventions.

Another important ingredient for success in treating the somatizing patients is to ask each time about their usual somatic symptoms. Of course, one should always be alert to new symptoms, since even somatizers do get sick. But after a brief laying on of hands by the physician, it is appropriate to ask the patients about their life circumstances and what is going on in their lives that is of special import.

Sometimes the physician is the patient's only confidant, as the complaining is off-putting to many families and friends. Often these somatizing patients lead lives in some disarray. Moreover, their somatizing symptoms have been a way of life. Since many of these patients use repression as one of their immature defenses, the clinician should not be surprised to find old clinic or hospital records with similar somatic complaints going back to childhood, although the patient may well not be aware of having such symptoms at such a young age.

CONVERSION DISORDERS

Internists typically are baffled by such patients' complaints, and neurologists are often made anxious by these patients' symptoms, which may simulate a serious neurological disorder yet without the relevant neurological signs. Indeed, about 25% of conversion disorder patients diagnosed as such by psychiatrists and neurologists on academic inpatient units do go on to develop, at a later date, a serious neurological disorder that, in retrospect, accounted for the unusual but still undiagnosed neurological condition.

Collaborative information from the conversion disorder patient's intimates is crucial to gaining an understanding of the psychosocial scene. Some aspect of the familial or occupational stress has become a precipitant to the patient's "psychic meltdown" and conversion. Such patients are using the defense of denial and repression, often showing some pleasure, or at least indifference, in the face of their somatic disability.

With a conversion disorder, some aspect of the recent past has been repressed and is unavailable to the patient for a considerable period of time. Clinicians treating patients with conversion disorders usually must spend an inordinate amount of time identifying the unacknowledged psychosocial pressures that these patients initially are unaware of. In an academic setting, before managed care and cost-accountability were issues, it would not be unusual for the clinician to spend an intensive 10 hours sorting through and gathering information and forming a relationship with the patient before psychological treatment orienting toward symptom removal and improvement in the psychosocial domain could really begin.

SOMATOFORM PAIN DISORDERS

The only health care workers that are pleased to see chronic pain patients are those that are working in an organized pain clinic, one that has multispecialty services to deal with the patient's biopsychosocial plight. Chronic pain is often very disabling and does not respond sufficiently to the usual somatic ministrations, such as oral opiates. After further thorough investigation for the medical etiology of the pain, a pain clinic is the ideal place for therapeutic trials of an opiate patch, acupuncture, local or brain electrical simulation, surgery, or referral to a specialized day treatment rehabilitation hospital program with individual/group psychotherapy plus couples and family therapy. Interestingly, clinical investigators have reported that unmedicated pain patients often have lower than normal levels of endorphins in their spinal fluid.

Somatoform pain disorder is characterized by the occurrence of one or more physical complaints for which appropriate medical evaluation reveals no explanatory physical pathology or pathological mechanism. When somatic pathology is present, the physical complaints are grossly in excess of what would be expected from the physical findings. In contrast to complaints from patients with pain disorder from a medical condition, somatoform pain disorder symptoms are often poorly described, nonvarying in intensity. The main clinical feature of somatoform pain disorder is that the pain cannot be fully attributed to a known medical disorder, with the pain causing significant distress, impairment, or both in social, academic, occupational, or other areas of function. Moreover, psychological factors are judged by the clinician to play an important role in the onset, severity, exacerbation, or maintenance of the pain. This disorder is often associated with nonresolvable psychosocial conflicts, and at times is associated with an early history of corporal punishment. Psychological treatment can be beneficial.

MENTAL HEALTH TREATMENT OF SOMATOFORM PAIN DISORDER AND PAIN DISORDER

Patients with chronic unremitting pain, with or without a determined psychological component, are living in their own private hell. For those patients that do not resolve their dilemma by suicide, there can be some optimism for improvement in pain. But suicide is a real risk for all patients in chronic severe intractable pain, especially when the patient gives up and feels given up on by his or her caregiver. Since pain is entirely subjective, there is no way of understanding the extent of the pain except by getting a report from the patient. A Visual Analogue Scale, with 0 being no pain and 10 being the most unbearable pain that one could experience, has been found helpful by clinicians in a variety of settings.

Withdrawal from opioids, if ineffective, coupled with the patient's keeping active and trying to get on with his or her life, is part of the psychoeducational approach to the pain patient. Goal setting is very important, with encouragement of early gradual return to normal activity even in the face of the pain. Family-centered treatment is often somewhat effective.

Antidepressants, whether the patient is depressed or not, can play a real role. The most recent of the serotonin and selective norepinephrine reuptake inhibitors (SNRIs), duloxetine, has based much of its extensive consumer-directed advertising on studies conducted on depressed patients with pain. Comprehensive care for patients in severe pain, whether it be somatoform pain or pain with or without any perceived psychological component, may be quite similar: support, pain medication if effective, family conflict resolution, and a push back to living life.

The goal is to continue to live life despite the pain, or to embrace the pain so that it is not the dominant feature of every moment. Training in relaxation, cognitive behavioral training with biofeedback, family therapy, counseling, dealing with the anxiety generated by the pain, seeking ways to avoid stressors, finding renewed meaning in life, decreasing the disability associated with the pain, and treatment of associated co-morbid conditions are all steps along the way toward the resumption of more normal living.

HYPOCHONDRIACAL DISORDERS

Hypochondriasis is a persistent though usually episodic anxiety concerning a medical condition, supposedly undetected despite much evaluation and considerable worry, that does not yield to rational explanation or persistent reassurance from physicians or family members. It is not uncommon for anyone to have some passing preoccupation with disease. Nor is it unusual for people to have intermittent, unfounded worries about medical illness. Medical students in particular often have brief runs of preoccupation with a morbid illness that will take their lives. This has been given the name of "medical student nosophobia."

But hypochondriacal disorder is more than a series of transient complaints of worry about a disease. It is a long-lasting condition characterized by obsessing about a disease that is coupled with considerable distress to the patient. Presumably because of the persistent intensity of the obsessing, there is also some dysfunction in the areas of living, loving, and working.

A clear majority of such patients also have another Axis I mental disorder, most likely depressive and anxiety disorders. In one general medical clinic 88% of all patients with hypochondriacal disorder had one or more concurrent psychiatric disorders. Many hypochondriacs also have Axis II personality disorders. However, it is rather unusual for hypochondriacs to show up in the mental health system solely for the purpose of treatment of hypochondriasis, since they rarely see their problems as having a mental basis. Like other somatoform disorder patients, hypochondriacs are high utilizers of medical services.

Of interest, some hypochondriacs actually are more aware of their internal bodily feelings. In the context of other family members' hypochondriasis, their own early childhood illness, or an anxiety disorder, sometimes a person with abdominal discomfort develops abdominal pain. Typically the disorder is exacerbated in a setting of a recent stressful event (e.g., the death of a close friend or relative). Then the "what if" of an anxious person becomes the "Do I have ... undetected cancer?" with obsessive preoccupation/rumination.

One survey reports that psychological treatments are far preferred by hypochondriacs willing to accept some form of treatment, rather than medication. But psychoanalytic and psychodynamic therapies have a poor track record with hypochondriacs. Regular appointments with a physician, perhaps even one practicing complementary and alternative medicine, have also been shown to be reassuring and of some benefit. The foundation of treatment seems to be a good therapeutic alliance in a clinician that is not repelled by the patient's frequent refocusing on disease constructs and requesting reassurances. A randomized controlled trial of referral to a psychiatrist and follow-up by the PCP, following an instructive letter to the PCP about diagnostic and therapeutic measures, resulted in a considerable decrease in health care costs without a decrease in patient satisfaction. Should the mental health clinician follow the patient, using a 14-item, simple self-report, the Whiteley Index (widely available on the web) is suggested. The Whitely Index facilitates following the course of the disorder over time.

There is emerging evidence that both cognitive behavior therapy and high doses of off-label SSRIs are effective in treatment, as is group therapy. Delusional hypochondriasis associated with a psychotic depression requires both an SSRI and a neuroleptic. Parasitosis in two double-blinded placebo-controlled studies showed pimozide (Orap) to be more effective than placebo.

Both cognitive therapy, to help identify thoughts that contribute to fears about illness, and behavioral stress management, including learning relaxation techniques, help people to avoid becoming so focused on their illness during stressful situations. Acupuncture, exercise, and good nutrition may also have a role.

Chapter 15

Working With the Patient With Mild Schizophrenia

In this quick-grab chapter, we focus on diagnostic and medication issues for outpatients with mild schizophrenia. The reason that we use *mild* with schizophrenia is that patients with severe and persistent mental illness that are burdened with schizophrenia are rarely best served in a private practice office setting.

TREATMENT ISSUES WITH PATIENTS WITH CHRONIC SEVERE SCHIZOPHRENIA

Patients with chronic mental illness (called CMI by many community mental health centers, as well as SPMI, for serious and persistent mental illness, by the Department of Veterans Affairs (VA)) usually have a multiplicity of social problems in living on a day-to-day basis with: being able to stay in an apartment in the community, being able to take care of hygiene and maintaining healthy nutrition, and getting to visits at the mental health clinic and the primary care physician's office. After five decades of modern psychopharmacology, functional outcomes have not yet substantially improved due to newer neuroleptics. Only about 20% of patients with schizophrenia can work independently. Traditional practice used to be only focused on control of positive symptoms until the multi-disciplinary "recovery focus" infused the field. This new development has certainly improved the quality of life for patients with schizophrenia.

Still there are myriad problems typically encountered in the treatment of patients with schizophrenia. For example, of first-episode patients, one-third are nonadherent with medication within six months. And most patients have at least periods of nonadherence.

Recent studies of medication compliance with electronically monitored pill bottles have demonstrated that both patients and prescribers grossly overestimate medication adherence.

Younger patients are at higher risk for nonadherence with medication, nonadherence for visits, denial of mental illness, depression,
poor quality of life, suicide, weight gain with metabolic complications, and extrapyramidal side effects.

Mental health care to a vast majority of such patients simply can't be
provided effectively within the context of the 20-minute hour unless
it is complemented by a strong team dedicated to dealing with the
complex psychosocial issues, such as housing, sheltered employment,
disability applications, Medicaid, Medicare, and Social Security
Income applications, plus transportation, food stamps, medications,
co-morbid substance abuse, and so forth.

Although some patients on clozapine (Clozaril) have a Lazarus-
like rebirth, this is often the exception and not the rule. Moreover,
most private practice office settings are not well suited to provide
biweekly intramuscular injections of depot neuroleptics, which
many patients need to decrease the likelihood of relapse. Finally,
schizophrenic patients that are doing rather well are still subject to
relapses that could very much overwhelm a private practice office.

Even if a very rich family can afford to pay fees for twice weekly
and PRN (as needed) visits without regard to insurance reimbursement, there are services that the public sector does better with than
the private sector. Family education, supported employment, assertive community treatment, and cognitive behavioral therapy are all
part of standard community mental health center treatment. For
example, state and VA mental health facilities offer integrated psychiatric and social support resources, plus case workers and the
ready access to an emergency team with active assertive treatment.

The recovery model is strongly supported in the public sector
with therapists, nurses, case workers, and psychiatrists in a team
model rarely, if ever, found in the private sector.

TREATMENT OF PATIENTS WITH MILD SCHIZOPHRENIA

Within the group of patients labeled with schizophrenia there still
exists perhaps one-third to one-fifth with a relatively good prognosis.
Characteristics are an illness of recent acute onset, good insight, a

high level of motivation to adhere to a medication regimen, and an understanding of the salience model of psychosis (where a flood of dopamine gives untoward causal meaning to certain unrelated events). Such patients usually have good social support and a ready resolution of the conflict that "short-circuited their (vulnerable) wires."

> Mrs. L is a 28-year-old psychiatric staff nurse at a private psychiatric hospital. She had a distant family member with schizophrenia with whom she had had no personal contact. After breaking up with a boyfriend with whom she had been living, she abruptly developed paranoid delusions of persecution coupled with agitation and sadness, but no hallucinations. She had poor concentration, and slept little. She had never abused alcohol or prescription drugs and never used illegal substances.
>
> She was hospitalized for a week but recovered rapidly after she was started on risperidone (Risperdal). She was given a discharge diagnosis of brief psychotic disorder. She returned to her normal baseline, and went back to her work as a floor nurse on a psychiatric unit within a month of onset of her first symptoms.
>
> Three months after the onset of her symptoms, she felt completely well and so stopped her risperidone on her own initiative. She did well at work and her mood remained euthymic, but she noted that toward the end of her daily shifts her write-ups tended to ramble and were confusing. Moreover, she began to feel vaguely threatened, although she knew there was no threat.
>
> When she consulted a psychiatrist in his private practice office, she appeared to be a vivacious and insightful woman with appropriate concerns. She was able to relate directly and warmly, with occasional appropriate humor. She was without depressive signs or symptoms. She thought that she might have schizophrenia and requested a trial on perphenazine (Trilafon), as this was a medication that was not given to any of the patients in her inpatient unit.
>
> She did well over the ensuing months. Then again on her own initiative she instigated a trial off medication to see if she really needed it. Three weeks later she returned to the office, having decided that she indeed did want to continue the medication, since off perphenazine her notes again were starting to become disorganized. She said: "I need this medication to provide me with more psychic glue." She did well on 4 to 8 mg of perphenazine and had no more episodes or dysfunction over the next five years.

Indeed for such good-prognosis patients one wonders about the correct diagnosis: brief psychotic episode, schizophreniform disorder, new-onset bipolar II illness presenting with a depressive episode, unacknowledged alcohol or PCP-precipitated episode, or schizoaffective disorder. But for 80 to 90% of schizophrenic patients, their diagnosis is not an issue for debate.

With psychotic episodes that are acute and quickly resolved, one sometimes looks to a family history of some Axis I disorder. But this is perilous since, given our current DSM-IV criteria, there still is considerable history overlap of schizophrenia and bipolar disorder in many families.

There are no clear-cut pharmacological guidelines about which medications to use for patients with mild schizophrenia. Patient preference informed by patient knowledge of short-term and long-term adverse effects should guide decision making. Obviously, the use of minimally effective dose is of importance to avoid deleterious outcomes. Adherence to a consistent regimen of a neuroleptic is important.

PHARMACOLOGICAL ISSUES INFORMED BY THE CATIE TRIAL

The now completed landmark NIMH-sponsored CATIE (Clinical Antipsychotic Trials of Intervention Effectiveness) trials have produced much information about the lack of effectiveness of current neuroleptics. In brief, CATIE was a $40 million 18-month study involving 1,460 participants at 57 different clinical sites in 24 states. The subjects were all outpatients receiving antipsychotic medication. All patients were deemed relatively stable, but were willing to enroll in the study in hopes of improvement. This effectiveness trial sought to be broadly representative of real-life settings, and as such included patients with physical or other mental health problems in addition to schizophrenia.

Upon entry to the study 42% of the patients already had the metabolic syndrome, presumably associated with the use of some neuroleptic medication, and 7% (100 patients) already had tardive dyskinesia. Drugs in the trial included second-generation antipsychotic agents (SGAs), with 320 cases entered into each of these four cells: olanzapine (Zyprexa), quetiapine (Seroquel), risperidone (Risperdal), and ziprasidone (Geodon). Additionally, 320 patients without tardive dyskinesia were entered into the cell of a first-generation antipsychotic agent, perphenazine (Trilafon). Treatment was otherwise randomized and double blinded without placebo. Patients on one of the SGAs that discontinued treatment due to lack of efficacy were randomly assigned to double-blind treatment with one of the other SGAs (50%) or clozapine (Clozaril) (50%).

The primary outcome measure for the study was *all cause treatment discontinuation*, reflecting the principal investigators' interest in efficacy and tolerability.

The biggest surprise of the study was that the older medication, perphenazine, was comparably effective to at least three of the SGAs, and not much worse than the SGA that did the best, olanzapine. Contrary to expectations, the older, less expensive medication, perphenazine, did not cause substantially more Parkinsonian-type side effects than the new drugs.

Nearly three-quarters of the patients discontinued their originally assigned medication before the end of the 18-month trial. Risperidone had the lowest rate of discontinuation due to intolerability (10%), followed by perphenazine, quetiapine, and ziprasidone (each 15%), with 18% quitting olanzapine. This last agent was associated with weight gain and increases in glycosylated hemoglobin, total cholesterol, and triglycerides. Weight gain of 7% or more occurred with olanzapine (30%), quetiapine (16%), risperidone (14%), and ziprasidone (7%). The agent aripiprazole (Abilify) was not included in the study, as it was not Food and Drug Administration (FDA) approved until 2002.

There were other side effects from these medications: Quetiapine had more anticholinergic side effects (31%) than the other agents, which were still in the 20 to 25% range. Only risperidone produced some hyperprolactinemia. There was no substantial QTc interval prolongation (an EKG-derived index or cardiac repolarization, which, if prolonged, indicates a potential vulnerability to a potentially fatal arrhythmia) with ziprasidone. There were also no cataracts associated with quetiapine, issues of previous concern in some reports.

BOTTOM LINE

Based on the findings of the CATIE study there is no "one size fits all" algorithm. Rather, the choice of neuroleptic should be governed by the prescribers' assessment of a patient's status and past history of response. Results from the CATIE trials showed that there was overall little improvement in psychosocial functioning in their study patients after 18 months. There was, however, modest improvement in psychosocial functioning for one-third of the patients that were able to continue on to finish the CATIE trial. The poor level of psychosocial improvement in this medication trial leads to the conjecture that substantial improvement would require intensive adjunctive psychosocial rehabilitation interventions.

Regarding side effects from SGAs, olanzapine, quetiapine, and risperidone in some patients were associated with some sedation and a foggy mental state, at least initially, whereas ziprasidone and aripiprazole were not. These same three SGAs are responsible for weight gain, but clozapine produces more.

Perhaps a third of patients on olanzapine will suffer severe weight gain. When a patient is consistently gaining a pound a week, a change of the SGA is probably warranted. Typically, patients with weight gain on other SGAs will lose some or all of that weight over time on aripiprazole, and even sometimes on ziprasidone. Weighing the patient on a weekly basis in the office, either at the onset of using an SGA or soon thereafter, is an important part of clinical care.

Risperidone was associated with impotence, lactation, or amenorrhea due to an elevation of serum prolactin levels (which can be measured routinely in clinical labs). Aripiprazole and ziprasidone may be able to reverse the dyslipidemias from other SGAs, although the research data on the benefit of these switches are still not conclusive.

SWITCHING FROM ONE ANTIPSYCHOTIC AGENT TO ANOTHER

For patients that are doing well on a neuroleptic, analysis of the CATIE data indicate that switching to improve symptom control may backfire. That is, those patients that did not have to switch from one medication to another as a result of the randomization process had better psychosocial outcomes.

Other clinical trials, however, indicate that some patients with a suboptimal outcome or intolerable side effects (sedation, weight gain, extrapyramidal side effects, abnormal laboratory data) may benefit when switched from one agent to another. One rationale for switching: as of yet there is no compelling data that ziprasidone or aripiprazole are associated with problems of increased weight, dyslipidemia, or problems with glucose metabolism. Another rationale for switching: since there may be some differences in improvement in cognition and in receptor affinity among the SGAs, it may be useful to try to switch from one to another of the SGAs to maximize the patient's recovery. In some outpatient clinics, switching patients on SGAs occurs in 30 to 50% of patients in a year.

There are two methods for switching: the slow crossover and the rapid crossover. With the slow crossover, the usual SGA is continued at a therapeutic dose as the new SGA is slowly titrated up over several weeks. After the new SGA attains maintenance dosage, the original SGA is discontinued. In the rapid crossover, the original SGA is gradually discontinued while another SGA is gradually titrated to a therapeutic dose. The slow crossover has been found to be more acceptable to patients and clinicians since there should be no issues of withdrawal symptoms from the initial SGA. Abrupt withdrawal is not recommended for patients on clozapine.

In effecting a switch, the clinician needs to be aware that there is a lag time before the initial SGA loses its therapeutic efficiency, but this lag time varies from patient to patient.

Therefore, the patient's clinical status on the replacement SGA, in determining the appropriate replacement level, may not be a reliable indicator of dosage necessary for relapse prevention. Thus, the patient's dose may need to be readjusted after the crossover is completed.

An individual approach is warranted here: Rapid taper or abrupt discontinuation may be necessitated due to medical problems such as agranulocytosis, neuroleptic malignant syndrome, or ketoacidosis. However, reemergent withdrawal dyskinesia or worsening of clinical symptoms may dictate reintroduction of the initial agent, followed by a descending switch, cross-titration, or any plateau switch method.

Since the patient's symptoms during a crossover may not be a good guideline to eventual dosage of the replacement SGA, it is best to use traditional dosing recommendations (15–30 mg of aripiprazole, 15–25 mg of olanzapine, 500–800 mg of quetiapine, 4.5–8 mg of risperidone, 120–180 mg of ziprasidone, and 350–500 mg of clozapine).

Chapter 16

Working With the Questionably Psychotic Patient

In this quick-grab chapter we focus on the term *psychotic*, which is used by clinicians in a variety of ways, so that its meaning, as it applies to a particular patient, is often blurred. Although *psychotic* implies having an impairment to assess reality, there are many gradations of clinical usage.

Some patients, thinking they are Jesus Christ, see all the world through a distorted prism.

Sometimes one imputes psychotic thinking to a patient using many neologisms, having thought blocking or "word salad," or even if the patient is unwilling to share his or her thoughts. Sometimes one hypothesizes that the patient is having visual hallucinations based on the patient's eyes tracking some object (unseen by the clinician) in a corner of the examining room. In such patients it is always safer to assume there is a dense psychosis, rather than questionable psychosis, and to plan accordingly for the safety of the patient and the clinician. These patients' judgment, insight, and behavior cannot be taken for granted.

On some occasions, a patient may talk openly about a delusional system (FBI, CIA, IRS, neighbors, and conspiracy). At times the patient may be quite "sane" in all other aspects, but for a circumscribed area of his or her life, and may even function very well at the job or with the family as long as decision making does not fall into the area of the delusional system. Such patients, if keeping their delusions to themselves, which is often the case, may not appear to be psychotic. Only by understanding the patient's mental experiences as well as activities of, and quality of, daily living, can one understand just how dense is a patient's psychotic experience. Some patients can become very aware of the nonreality of their otherwise real-seeming hallucinations, but this certainly is not often the case.

> Dr. M, an elderly practicing neurologist being treated for bipolar II depressions, had been started on lithium three weeks earlier to augment his Imipramine. Early one Saturday morning he rushed to his Beacon Street condominium window to see the marching band that he heard in the street below. Seeing no such band, he realized that he was having an auditory hallucination and might be getting toxic from his lithium and imipramine. He called for an appointment, had his blood drawn that day, stopped his lithium, and was seen two days later in the office; his lithium was restarted, but at a lower level.

The presence of a hallucination by definition means psychotic, but in the case above, the patient had almost all his reality testing intact, and he showed very good judgment.

Some depressed patients may report shadowy figures on the periphery of their visual fields. Others may begin to hear voices that call out their name, or a knock on the front door with no one there. These patients, if they reflect, usually realize that "the mind is playing tricks" on them. They may not make the next connection that their depression is going from mild to more severe. Still, the presence of auditory, visual, or other hallucinatory experiences in the context of a major depressive disorder is sufficient to add the term *psychotic* to the diagnosis of major depressive disorder. As such, the adding of a neuroleptic to an antidepressant agent would be the appropriate treatment. Such patients may or may not have delusional hopelessness, so it is best to check for this.

The nature of the patient's transference to the clinician may vary widely, to a considerable extent based on how densely psychotic the patient is. With the schizophrenic patient, especially when not fully medicated, transference fantasies may be exceedingly real, and potentially very dangerous to the clinician if the patient decides to act out his or her beliefs, for example, attacking the mental health worker for some imagined unacceptable trait or action.

PHARMACOLOGICAL PRINCIPLES

Adherence with the treatment plan may also vary widely with the density of the psychotic process. Up to half of *inpatients* do not swallow their nurse-administered psychoactive medications. Medical patients without psychiatric disorders usually have variable to poor compliance with medications that need to be taken more than once per day.

Patients with mild schizophrenia would seem to be more likely to take their medications if their ego functioning is intact. By contrast, it is probable that patients preoccupied with a dense psychosis do not believe they have mental illness. As such, they will not be very adherent in taking various oral medications. Such instances call for depot medication or careful monitoring of therapeutic levels of oral medications: lithium, valproic acid (Depakote), carbamazepine (Tegretol), and topiramate (Topamax), plus tricyclic antidepressants imipramine, desipramine, and nortriptyline. These blood levels are readily available and can help the assessment of compliance.

Working With the Adolescent Patient

In this quick-grab chapter, we address how to approach and assess the adolescent patient. If one were to listen closely to the parents of an adolescent *without* any psychiatric diagnosis or major functional difficulties as they describe their child's recent emotional state, one would hear terms such as: *moody, emotional lability, impulsive behavior, irritability, extremes of fad behavior, irresponsible, conflict with* [an authority figure] *coming out of nowhere, reckless driving/accident prone, secret substance abuse, poor judgment,* and *raging at limit setting.*

A clinician used to dealing only with adults would think that the individual so described must have some sort of major mental illness. Yet these terms also describe normal adolescents. There is an old saying: "Adolescence is not a disease, it may just seem that way." The clinician needs to be able to relate to the adolescent in a way quite different than from that of relating to an adult patient. Thus, any psychiatric illness complicating adolescence is just that much more complicated as a treatment issue, and may well need a longer time in treatment to heal.

How should the clinician relate to an adolescent? There certainly is no greater test of a clinician's authenticity in such a relationship. Being a "phony" will get detected right away and will sour any therapeutic alliance. Since all other adults may be labeled as "heavy," "intrusive," "overly probing," or "obnoxious," the clinician needs to show concern while also being rather informal. When confronted with personal and other questions, the clinician should try to be forthcoming rather than deflect the patient's questions.

N, an 18-year-old high school senior, was admitted to a partial hospital program with an affective disorder. She was very depressed, was isolating, had trouble with activities of daily living, had skipped school for two weeks, and was not bathing or taking care of herself. She was sleeping too much and was quite irritable. Although she gave straightforward if limited answers to questions, she refused to talk about her suicidal ideation, if any.

After the impasse about discussing suicidality, the interviewer shifted gears. The patient inspected the psychiatrist's office and then wanted to know about the children in pictures on the psychiatrist's desk and the wall calendar. She wanted to know if the psychiatrist was still married. She wanted to know how old the psychiatrist was.

The psychiatrist answered these queries in a friendly and nondefensive fashion. When the history taking resumed, N opened up. She said that her suicidal thoughts had been quite strong. She had heretofore never revealed how ill she was and how frightened she was because of it.

One may also judiciously use a small amount of humor to "lighten up" the heavy situation. Developing a positive rapport with the patient initially is more important than getting a comprehensive history. This assumes that there will be other times in the near future to gather data.

ASSUMPTIONS TO USE IN TALKING WITH AN ADOLESCENT

1. The patient is sexually active, or has been.
2. The patient needs some degree of recognition of his or her autonomy.
3. There need to be clear reassurances about privacy in the doctor-patient relationship.
4. Chronological age does not necessarily represent the developmental stage of emotional maturity.

Chapter 18

Working With the Elderly Patient

This quick-grab chapter will look at ways that the elderly mind processes data. Every clinician can spot full-blown dementia or severe depression. Most good textbooks are full of suggestions about treatment. So this chapter will focus on relevant information to help the clinician deal with a major issue: How is the elderly person thinking and processing experiences? Is the patient really dementing, or does he or she just show normative aging? Is the patient grieving? Is the patient toxic from some otherwise helpful medication? Can the patient or the family benefit from some type of psychotherapy?

Pediatricians remind us that children are not just short adults. But the elderly are much like adults, except more so. They have more stories to tell and may have more wisdom than young adults. According to the first director of the National Institute on Aging, Gene Cohen, MD, functional magnetic imaging shows that, when confronted with an intellectual task, the younger mind responds using either the left or right side of the brain. However, the older mind responds to the challenge by using both sides of the brain. In a talk at the Cosmos Club in 2008, Cohen asserted, "In middle age we begin to go on all-wheel drive. We have the capacity to look at the same information in a different way." Interpersonal problem solving is actually strengthened for older people compared to younger adults.

ANATOMY IS DESTINY, TO SOME EXTENT

Not all information on cognitive functioning in the elderly is upbeat. Although there is not a decrease in crystallized intelligence, there

147

is general slowing of cognitive functioning, starting in the 50s and 60s. Within the cortex, the prefrontal lobes are disproportionately affected by aging, as is the subcortical monoamine cell population, which connects to the frontal lobes. The temporo-parietal association areas are less impacted, as is the case with the globus pallidus, the paleocerebellum, the sensory cortices, and the pons.

Neurotransmitters diminish as the brain itself shrinks. There is a decrease in perceptual acuity and spatial functioning, which can place a processing overload in circumstances that once presented little challenge. White matter tracks, for example, connecting the frontal lobes to brain storage areas, change, so that information takes longer to process.

The decline in working memory (short-term memory with the ability to manipulate information held in conscious memory) may place limits on other complex cognitive skills. Forward digit span recall in the 30s is typically seven digits, but by the 80s it is six digits. But recollection *with interference* shows more of an age differential. On tasks such as delayed five-minute recall of three or four single words, older persons recall less, although their performance does improve with repetition. Older adults require more effort in active encoding and retrieval.

Incidental memory (What color was the dress the hostess was wearing at the dinner last night?) may be equal for young and old. Prospective memory in a laboratory setting is better for younger than older adults. But in a naturalistic setting, older adults' memory may be better than younger adults', since the older adults are more used to using reminder notes or cues.

Names take longer to recall with aging. But the elderly need not worry about these "senior moments" unless they are having trouble recalling recent events and conversations. Moreover, Alzheimer's is not the only cause for decreased mental activity: Depression, alcohol abuse, thyroid problems, vitamin deficiencies, and hormone deficiencies are very treatable causes of memory difficulties.

MEDICATIONS AND MENTATION

Medications can impair mental functioning (see Table 18.1). The explanation for the sensitivity of the elderly to medication is based mostly on somatic changes. For example, the elderly have a relative loss of body water and lean body mass, so that there is an increased

Table 18.1 Common Medications That May Impact Cognitive Function

Antihistamines: diphenhydramine (Benadryl)

Anti-parkinsonian agents: trihexyphenidyl (Artane), benztropine (Cogentin)

Anti-motion sickness: meclizine (Antivert)

Benzodiazepines: lorazepam (Ativan), clonazepam (Klonopin), temazepam
(Restoril), diazepam (Valium)

Beta-blockers: propranolol (Inderal)

Digitalis: digoxin (Lanoxin)

Lithium: (Eskalith, Lithobid)

Narcotics: acetaminophen plus oxycodone (Percocet), acetaminophen plus
hydrocodone (Vicodan)

Steroids: prednisone

concentration of drugs that are typically distributed in body water
(e.g., lithium is distributed in the body water space, while digitalis
is distributed in the lean body mass). On the other hand, drugs
that are distributed in adipose tissue have a larger apparent volume
in many elderly, and thus will attain a lower plasma concentration. Since the serum albumen, which tightly binds some drugs,
is decreased by about 20% in the elderly, drugs such as warfarin
(Coumadin) or furosemide (Lasix) may be more free to go to action
sites at a higher concentration, with a greater drug effect. Finally,
renal excretion of drugs, measured by the glomerulo filtration rate
(GFR), declines 1% per year after age 30, so some drugs, such as
lithium, may not be cleared out as quickly in the elderly.

AGE-ASSOCIATED MEMORY IMPAIRMENT AND
MILD COGNITIVE IMPAIRMENT

The prevalence of age-associated memory impairment (AAMI) is
estimated to be 40% for those in their 50s and 85% for those in
their 80s and older. AAMI is a stable condition reflecting normal
aging. Mild cognitive impairment (MCI), however, is not necessarily stable. It is defined as a condition in which individuals have
greater memory problems than people normally do at a particular
age, but yet memory problems do not significantly (yet) effect their
functioning. That is, MCI involves cognitive impairment that is
objectively demonstrable, but does not seriously impact activities
of daily living. In seniors, over half of persons with MCI go on to

develop dementia after five years. Of course, the clinician should be aware of less likely causes of MCI, such as depression or other psychiatric disorders, metabolic or medical disorders, substance abuse, medication, or physical trauma. Neurologists consider detection of MCI to be important, since those individuals with MCI that progress to Alzheimer's disease (AD) can then be treated as early as possible.

If MCI is suspected, frequently used very brief tests of mentation, such as the Mini Mental Status Exam (MMSE) and the Six Item Orientation-Memory-Concentration Test, are not really sensitive enough. However, the Montreal Cognitive Assessment test (MoCA) can detect early AD with 100% sensitivity and 87% specificity. The MoCA was developed to detect MCI, and may now be the only screening tool available to distinguish between persons that have MCI and those that are normal for their age. It takes 10 minutes to administer, involves 30 measures, and is available for free at www.mocatest.org.

Simpler and briefer screening tools include the WORLD test. The patient is asked to spell that word *world* both forward and backward, then arrange the word's letters in alphabetical order. The test is scored as correct or incorrect. It has a sensitivity of 85% and a specificity of 88% for AD. When a highly educated patient fails the test, more formal testing is appropriate.

There is also the One Minute Naming Test: asking the patient to name as many animals, for example, as possible within one timed minute. If more than 21 animals are named, the patient is OK. But if less than 15 animals are named, the patient is likely to be cognitively impaired, with 20 times increased likelihood of developing AD.

Finally, there is the Mini-Cog, which takes two to four minutes to administer. The patient is asked to recall three words after drawing a picture of a clock. If the patient has no difficulty in recalling those three words, dementia is unlikely. If the patient can recall only one or two words, then the level of accuracy of the clock drawing becomes definitive. If the patient is unable to recall any of the words, dementia is likely and more formal testing should be initiated. If the patient responds positively to prompting, for example, a reminder of a category of a word used, like *animal* or *flower*, this is evidence of some capacity for recall. The Mini-Cog's sensitivity and specificity approaches that of the Mini Mental Status, which has been criticized as being too influenced by patients' educational level.

There are a number of other tests that have some predictive capacity for cognitive decline. Several scientific groups have developed simple identification of common odors (lemon, vanilla, leather, lilac, etc). In one study, risk of developing MCI increased over time as odor identification decreased below the average detection rate (8/12). A minimally invasive optical test, the interior laser ophthalmoscope, can readily determine the presence and extent of amyloid beta proteins in the ocular lens, which mirrors the amyloid in the brain in AD. Various brain imaging techniques now are coming online to detect the likelihood or presence of AD.

WORKING WITH THE ELDERLY

Working with the elderly is time-consuming. They have more illnesses to try to remember. They take more medications. There are even more medication trials of unknown medications that they cannot recall. Their charts are so heavy they cause us wrist pain to carry. They walk with us, but much more slowly. And, of course, they may remind us of loved, or not so loved, parents and other elderly relatives.

The biodiversity of body types and bodily health after age 60 continues to be amazing. Although there is a decreased variability in mental functioning with higher levels of education, there is an increased variability in health status associated with being depressed, medically ill, having weakened muscle strength, and being female.

For some, 70 is the new 50, and 90 the new 65. But for others, 59 is the new 60, or 70. If at age 40 we finally get the face that we deserve, at age 70 we get the health that we have worked on impacted by the genes that we inherited.

So, to know one elder is to know one elder. There is no place that better demonstrates this biodiversity of aging than 40th or 50th college reunions. Many classmates that show up are sprightly and fit, but some other classmates look like they came from a different, older generation.

Retirement is another chronologically timed event, and with some exceptions, most over 65 or 70 do retire, at least partially, if they can afford it. In the context of retirement, relationships also can show wear and tear. The aphorism "We marry for life but not for lunch" needs to be seriously discussed long before retirement is contemplated.

PERSONALITY TRAITS IN THE ELDERLY

There is an adage that the personalities of the elderly are similar to those of younger adults, only more so. Research studies demonstrate that desirable traits outweigh undesirable traits through middle age and early old age, regarding introversion-extroversion, psychological tempo, assertiveness, and hostility. Personality traits seem to be stable throughout adult life. However, the increased vulnerability that accompanies aging may amplify neurotic traits, increasing susceptibility to an elder's worries about health. Thus, it may be more difficult to reassure the elder using objective results.

Even though Freud thought that intensive work should not be considered for those patients over 40, experience shows that the elderly can work on issues of insight, personal growth, grieving, and couple communication. Granted, currently the elderly come from backgrounds where seeing a psychiatric clinician carries more stigma than for the young, but elderly patients rapidly put aside feelings of stigma when it appears that substantial improvement in quality of life can be accomplished.

> Mr. O is a 94-year-old retired lawyer, married for the past 60 years, but with growing marital discord since he retired as chairman of his firm 22 years ago. At that time, so that his wife could also retire from being a homemaker, at his suggestion he took over the task of housecleaning. She was never satisfied with how he performed these tasks, as they did not approach her perfectionistic standards. Over the years he became gradually more dour.
>
> He would not admit to being depressed, but he began to dwell on death as a good outcome for himself. He did admit to his primary care physician (PCP) that he was having low energy, was irritable, and felt worthless. His PCP tried him on 20 mg of citalopram (Celexa), which had neither main nor side effects. The patient discontinued this medication on his own after a month.
>
> Since he also had problems with chronic insomnia, his PCP had also treated him with amitriptyline (Elavil), then lorazepam, and finally zolpidem (Ambien). He also had had mild hypertension and radical resection of prostatic carcinoma many years ago but was otherwise in robust good physical health with a solid exercise program in his well-outfitted home gym.
>
> One evening after an argument with his wife, he impulsively took all the remaining zolpidem in what he later considered to be a bona fide suicide attempt. When he could not be roused the next morning, his wife called 911.

He was taken to a nearby ICU for four days, then transferred to the psychiatric unit, for his first ever psychiatric hospitalization.

On the psychiatric inpatient unit, he related that he was surprised, but glad, to be alive. He was apologetic for the attempt, and hoped to reconcile with his spouse. He answered questions quickly and was very friendly. His MMSE was 27/30. (He had problems recalling the name of his county of residence and difficulty accurately copying a design of two pentagonal figures. He could recall only two of three objects after one minute.) He was started on venlafaxine (Effexor XR) and discharged as having a single episode of major depressive disorder and an obsessive compulsive personality disorder.

Transferred to the partial hospital program, over the next week, he was rapidly titrated up to 150 mg of Effexor XR without any apparent side effects. But after a week on that dosage he felt wobbly, so the dose was decreased to 112.5 mg. His sleep and spirits improved remarkably. His spouse rather suddenly became appreciative of what he had been trying to do (sharing domestic chores), and they began to get along better than ever before.

Assessment by the occupational therapist determined that he was able to problem solve, take care of his own medications, and had only minor short-term memory problems. With minimal psychotherapeutic intervention, their communication opened up considerably. By discharge three weeks after the attempt, he was looking forward to going home and doing some volunteer work in the community.

LOSSES

The elderly have had to experience more losses of friends, family, and even adult children than seems possible to bear. The elderly often first read the obituary columns in the newspaper and the necrology columns in college alumni bulletins. Prospective studies of new widows and widowers find that about half cope with the loss of a spouse with only minor levels of distress, without loss of self-esteem, inappropriate guilt, or suicidal ideation. Chronic grief lasting more than two years is rare. However, those with few friends or with estranged children tend to have a harder time adjusting to widowhood. Siblings become increasingly important with aging. Being involved in multiple social roles (worker, spouse, grandparent, caregiver) also leads to higher levels of satisfaction and feeling of self-sufficiency.

Mrs. P is an 86-year-old woman, widowed a year ago, and moved by her children to California, to be near her older daughter following their selling the family house and car. She was admitted to a partial hospital program two weeks after her return home for a brief visit with the chief complaint of: "I'm here to get my head on straight, to feel better about myself, and to share the agonizing losses that I have had."

She had had a history of recurrent depressions since early in her marriage with three psychiatric hospitalizations, the last a decade ago. After the death of her husband, she did receive much community support from friends and from church, but she described herself as being in a daze. She made frequent frantic calls to her children and friends. Suddenly after her husband's death, she seemed quite unable to take care of her financial and personal needs. She was referred to a psychiatrist for an evaluation because of her disorganized state, but she left before her evaluation was complete. Her MMSE was recorded as 29/30, and no diagnosis was made other than pathological grieving. The psychiatrist recommended that she continue on the mirtazepine (Remeron), buspirone (Buspar), and zolpidem that she had been taking for many years.

In the partial hospital program she described her marriage in matter-of-fact ways, that each partner was dependent on the other, and in that way they had done very well together. There was a strong maternal family history of depression. All three of her adult children had needed psychiatric treatment when they were in middle school or high school. Two were very estranged and the third, a daughter nearby in California with power of attorney over her financial affairs, made occasional dutiful visits to her assisted living facility, but often pointed out that her money at some point was going to run out and she would not sacrifice her family's well-being for the patient.

Mrs. P felt trapped in that facility, not allowed to do things for herself, deprived of opportunities to attend cultural events, and basically infantilized.

She hated the place, felt a prisoner there, and had not attempted to make any friends despite being urged to do so.

She reported that she had always been a nervous person, but that her short-term memory had improved considerably in the past six months, and that she no longer was in a daze all the time. She became so homesick to return to her native town and did so, but during her month-long visit there, while staying with a friend, including her time in the partial hospital program, she had not initiated any activity to secure an independent living facility in her native town.

In the partial hospital program she began to accept that her own passivity, and the lack of real family support in her old town had prevented her from developing a plan for better living. She accepted, reluctantly, a plan to return to California. She agreed to do a cash flow analysis with her daughter to see what type of independent living facility she could best afford. She decided not look to her children for the kind of support that she pined for, and to begin to build a life for herself.

The patient's medications were not changed, but after five days her outlook had brightened considerably and she looked forward, albeit with mixed feelings, to redeveloping her own life.

TAKE-HOME POINTS IN DEALING WITH THE ELDERLY

1. The elderly constitute a group of individuals with widely divergent biological ages and relative youthfulness or elderliness despite similar birthdates.
2. To be elderly means that one has experienced many losses associated with this phase of life (working role, autonomy, home, mobility independence, finances, and health) and often considerable grieving.
3. To work with the elderly for an intake takes far more time than for a younger person, as the elderly have experienced far more medical and life-changing experiences, some of which may prove to be relevant to their chief complaint.
4. Dementia, delirium, and depression are common, but not normal consequences of aging.
5. Pharmacodynamics and pharmacokinetics become more than just small paragraphs in a textbook when dealing with the elderly. Their changed body water composition, renal excretion rates, and a plethora of medications make a more sophisticated knowledge of pharmacology necessary.
6. We must remember President John F. Kennedy's famous quote: "It is not enough to add years to one's life … one must also add life to those years."

Chapter 19

Working With the Borderline Personality Patient

In this quick-grab chapter we focus on a disorder that is more prevalent than schizophrenia, and may be more so than bipolar disorder. Yet the general public has little if any information about borderline personality disorder. Ten million Americans, or 2% of the adult population, have borderline personality disorder, three-quarters of them women. An extraordinarily large number of these people go undiagnosed for years before receiving proper treatment. But in the words of Otto Kernberg, MD in the video "Back from the Edge": "Once they begin getting the right treatment and support, many people with borderline personality disorder can sustain loving relationships and enjoy meaningful careers."

The symptoms of this disorder include instability of mood, thinking, behaving, interpersonal relationships, and self-image. These patients have a very difficult time controlling their impulses. This is particularly the case when under stress, especially when under negative emotional impact. Very recently functional magnetic resonance imaging (MRI) research in a laboratory setting has begun for the first time to delineate the underlying dysfunction in certain brain structures for these patients, compared to well-matched normal controls.

Borderlines and healthy controls were tasked with pushing a button for words printed in a standard font, but not in an italicized font. There were very few italicized words. Since there were few italicized words, all subjects quickly achieved the habit of pushing the button—impulse control was required *not* to push the button. The words were mostly positive or neutral, but sometimes they were negative. As you might expect, the borderlines pushed the button more when they were not supposed to, especially when the italicized words had a negative connotation.

When scanned with functional MRI, those with borderline personality, in comparison to the normal controls, did not display the expected decreased orbito-frontal and subgenual cingulate cortices activity usually associated with emotional regulation, nor did they display inhibition of limbic system structures, including the amygdale, when confronted with negative words on trials where they were not supposed to push a button.

In summary, borderlines displayed brain responses associated with *automatic* emotional reactions rather than using brain mechanisms that would *regulate* these emotions.

CLINICAL PRESENTATION

Over time, borderline patients have many highly emotional symptoms. But when such a patient is in a stable phase, the mental status may be unremarkable. For example, if you were to meet a borderline person at a cocktail party, you might well be impressed by the nice, caring, and vulnerable person with a vibrant personality and a kind persona. Only on finding out about the multiple relationships and chaotic lifestyle can one begin to suspect the diagnosis of borderline personality disorder.

During the initial intake interview for outpatient treatment, the patient often presents as an organized, attractive person with some waif-like, appealing qualities and an openness to share many aspects of his or her previous chaotic relationships. Although some of these patients may give lurid histories of polymorphous, perverse pan-sexuality, this certainly is not always the case.

When inquiring about the patient's lifestyle, the clinician learns that the borderline constantly demanded attention, cannot stand to be alone, and is often difficult to live with and work with. There is much emotional dysregulation. Often he or she is chronically angry, quick to take offense, easily depressed, and makes unreasonable demands on friends and family. He or she may throw tantrums and make suicide threats. The person may feel incomplete, empty, and may be entirely dependent on another, but then suddenly is quite able to break away.

About a quarter of patients with borderline personality disorder may have posttraumatic stress disorder (PTSD) from sexual/emotional abuse as a child, but childhood abuse or neglect is not associated with all cases of borderline personality disorder.

Although impulsivity and aggression can occur in the absence of a major depressive episode, depression makes everything in the borderline worse, and up to 60% of borderline patients have such episodes. Unlike the depressed patient without borderline traits, the depressive episodes of some borderlines are much more responsive to external events.

Family histories of borderline patients are usually replete with psychopathology, often with affective disorders. Many theories of etiology relate both environment and heredity in borderline patients.

IN TREATMENT

During the early phases of outpatient treatment, the patient more often than not idealizes the therapist, but the opposite, for no obvious reason, may also occur when the patient requests transfer to another clinician.

After several sessions of establishing a relationship, the patient may feel relieved when the clinician decides to clarify the patient's diagnosis by reading directly the criteria for borderline personality disorder from DSM-IV. Patients are usually comforted to learn that they have a known medical condition, not a character defect, one that has established treatments.

When borderline patients become forthcoming and calm, they will often describe themselves as feeling empty. Most problematic for the clinician are the borderline's threats and gestures of potential lethality, often impulsive but in a setting of threatened loss. The self-injurious behavior, including cutting or burning, bingeing, alcoholism, or drugs, sometimes is an attempt to keep in touch with the self, or avoid the psychic pain.

Borderlines often regress on a psychiatric unit, only to rapidly improve within a few days of being transferred to a state hospital. In a general hospital unit, a borderline's behavior usually rapidly splits the nursing staff, often with large staff meetings to work out a consistent plan to deal with such a patient. Toward the time for discharge for a medical condition, it is not surprising if the patient behaves in ways to undermine discharge: picking at bandages, infecting wounds, drinking mouthwash, faking an elevation of temperature by stealing a thermometer, then rubbing it to raise the temperature and replacing it in time to be read by the nurse as elevated.

PSYCHOLOGICAL TREATMENT OF
THE BORDERLINE PATIENT

Acknowledging the patient's distress and validating his or her feelings is an essential part of the treatment. Helping the patient to learn how to de-escalate out-of-control feelings is also very important. Marsha Linehan, PhD's, work on dialectic behavior therapy is highly regarded by the field.

A common feature of borderlines is their exquisite sensitivity to the nuances of interpersonal relationships. Perhaps their problems with prior interpersonal difficulties have primed them for this. Such an exquisitely sensitive "radar" often allows such a patient to be more quickly in touch with the therapist's countertransference than the therapist is. Distortions of the therapeutic or other relationships are to be expected, especially in times of stress. Splitting, devaluation, projection, and denial—all primitive defense mechanisms—keep cropping up.

John Clarkin, PhD, and Otto Kernberg, MD, have demonstrated that many different approaches from skilled practitioners seem to help the borderline patient. Dr. Clarkin's project featured a head-to-head 12-month trial with 90 patients, typical of those seen in clinical practice and treated by community practitioners in private offices. Patients were randomly assigned to transference-focused psychotherapy, dialectic behavior therapy, and supportive therapy.

Only transference-focused therapy brought about significant changes in impulsivity, irritability, verbal assault, and direct assault. Both transference-focused therapy and dialectic behavior therapy did better than supportive therapy in reducing suicidality. All three treatments, however, brought about positive change in multiple domains to about an equivalent extent.

As Glen Gabbard, MD, summing up the literature, mused (2007): "Could it be that any thoughtful, systematic approach to borderline personality disorder, based on our knowledge of the disorder, is potentially helpful, whatever its theoretical underpinnings or technical approach?" If so, this might confirm the nonspecificity of the effects of psychotherapy for this disorder. Or it could be that different types of psychotherapies work in different ways but contribute to overall improvement.

PSYCHOPHARMACOLOGICAL TREATMENT
OF THE BORDERLINE PATIENT

The peripsychotic, depressive, aggressive, or impulsive symptoms sometimes require pharmacological intervention. It is not quite the case that every drug used on bipolar or unipolar patients has had some positive results with the borderline personality disorder, but it appears to be nearly so. In some cases, it is prudent to use low doses of neuroleptics; in other cases, it may be wise to use high doses of antidepressants, and switch from one to another in search of efficacy, especially when the patient has a co-morbid affective disorder.

The 2001 APA practice guidelines, available at www.psych.org, devotes 11 pages to evidence about the pros and cons of medications for the borderline, including antidepressants from all classes, mood stabilizers, and neuroleptics. More recent reports show some success with those antiepileptic drugs sometimes used for the treatment of bipolar disorder. As usual, the prescriber is choosing an off-label use of medication based on the patient's symptoms, potential side effects, and patient preferences.

Chapter 20

Working With the Mildly Mentally Retarded Patient

In this quick-grab chapter we focus on aspects of treating mildly mentally retarded patients. These intellectually challenged patients can be very gratifying to work with, as long as the clinician uses a simple, straightforward communication style. Words should be purposefully kept to one or two syllables, and the rate of speech should not be too fast. Since the mentally retarded by definition are slow learners, usually important psychodynamic points need to be repeated slowly (without condescension) several times. The mildly mentally retarded are quite capable of benefiting from insight-oriented psychotherapy, on a once every two weeks or once a month basis. Often the insights may seem quite elemental to the therapist but can have quite a profound effect on the patient. But the "Aha!" the patient has when he or she gains insight into a vexing problem is a wonderful event to behold.

Strong positive transference often emerges and is apparent after a few sessions when the patient's shyness in the presence of a stranger gives way to appreciation. He or she appreciates being treated with considered attention and respect.

Sometimes the developmentally disabled patient will have somewhat garbled speech or mannerisms that are initially (and sometimes later) difficult for the clinician to interpret but are well understood by the caregiver. There may also be some problems of behavior that the patient does not see as ego-dystonic, but that the staff finds close to intolerable.

Also, there may be some patterns of behavior that the staff can predict as preceding a behavioral or emotional escalation—hence the reason for the visit. Such a session could be quite problematic for the uninitiated clinician to handle successfully alone. Hence, collaborative care is essential, and staff/parents are very appreciative of it. Collaborative information sources are essential. Typically, a mentally retarded person will be accompanied to, and into, the session by one or several caregivers from the group home, or by a parent. At least during the initial evaluation sessions, it is important to have these caregiving adults present for most or probably all of the session to help inform or interpret.

The patient may well be very anxious in the initial evaluation sessions, since many mentally retarded patients do quite poorly with change, and a trip from home to an unknown doctor is a great change. These patients do not have access to the usual mature ego defense mechanisms for binding their anxiety.

Paranoia, depression, hypomania, hoarding, compulsive rituals, and exposing oneself—these problems are rarely masked. The mentally retarded are usually quite up front with their feelings, as they are with their shame and guilt, their preferences, infatuations, and antipathies. According to the Association for Retarded Citizens, the most prevalent mental disorders are schizophrenia, organic brain syndrome, adjustment disorders, personality disorders, depression, and behavioral problems. About 20 to 35% of the mentally retarded that live in the community suffer from some type of psychiatric disorder.

At times, in an established relationship, toward the end of a session, a mentally retarded patient may request that the clinician see him or her alone, without the community caregiver present, but this is rather unusual. Most of the mildly mentally retarded live in group settings surrounded by their caregivers and peers, so the prospect of privacy is often rather unfamiliar and not as cherished as it is with the usual patient.

Mental retardation is an Axis II diagnosis, with mild, moderate, severe, and profound subtypes in *Diagnostic and Statistical Manual of Mental Disorders* (DSM-IV). But for those working in the field, the preferred term is *developmental disability*, and those patients with both an intellectual disability and a psychiatric diagnosis are usually referred to as having a dual disability.

Chapter 21

Working With the Suicidal Patient

In this quick-grab chapter, we focus on some of the essential management pointers when suicide is, or may be, an issue.

PSYCHIATRIC ILLNESS HAS A HIGH DEGREE OF MORBIDITY AND MORTALITY

Resident training directors learned that, based on pre-selective serotonin reuptake inhibitor (SSRI) data, one in six psychology trainees and one in three psychiatric residents experienced the suicide of a patient during training, according to a 2007 presentation made to them by Eric Plakun, MD, director of admissions at Austen Riggs Center. Whatever the rate is now, such a sentinel event is traumatic for the resident, elicits powerful emotional responses, and has an impact on the program as a whole.

Some say that there are only two types of clinicians—those who have experienced the death of a patient, and those who will. It certainly is an occupational hazard, one that we all hope to avoid.

Were some of these suicides avoidable? Perhaps. One always can second-guess and use 20/20 hindsight. But a determined help-repudiator whose depression is not so severe as to paralyze him or her can outwit experienced and conscientious clinicians and wear down loving and devoted family members. Such lethally determined patients can be ever alert to every possible opportunity to suicide.

The essential feature of working with the suicidal patient, from the clinician's perspective, is that one tries to do the essentials conscientiously. One constantly holds out hope and helps the healthy part of the patient to hang on to life, even when it does not seem so

Table 21.1 Potentiating Factors for Suicide

Life crisis
Agitation (perturbation)
Sleep loss
Panic/anxiety
Current substance intoxication
Hopelessness
Ready access to weapon
Access to other lethal means
  (especially firearms with ammunition)

Table 21.2 Mitigating Factors for Suicide

Positive therapeutic alliance
Interpersonal relationships/support
Hopefulness
Spirituality
Access to stable housing
Capacity for self-regulation
Verbalizing reasons to live

precious. One maintains contact and is alert to countertransference issues, newly emerging crises, and instances in which the patient feels hopeless and given up on by caregivers. The clinician must be aware of, and help to treat, perturbation, which can weaken the strongest link to life. One is also aware of both the current potentiating factors that make suicide more likely and the mitigating factors that make suicide less likely: all this in the context that suicide is an extraordinarily hard act to predict, even by the patient that is in the act of doing it (Tables 21.1 and 21.2).

It is best that each patient's suicide be accorded a psychological autopsy, protected by the peer review, and thus not available to legal discovery. This can be done through the auspices of the local chapter of the Psychiatric Society, the hospital, or some other organization that is set up to do peer reviews. The spirit of such inquiry is nonjudgmental, with the focus on learning about how the patient lived and how the patient died. Was anything done that should not have been? Was anything not done that could have been? In retrospect, was this death inevitable? It is truly impossible to tell prospectively if the patient is going to be a "croaker."

The clinician should express sorrow to the family for the outcome and participate in (free) post-vention services for family members if they should so desire. One should offer one's authentic condolences without self-criticism. There should not be a spectacle of *mea culpa* and apologies, as your malpractice risk manager will tell you. But we can all learn something from the death of a person, whether by suicide or natural causes.

CRITERIA FOR MANDATORY HOSPITALIZATION FOLLOWING A SUICIDE ATTEMPT

Since there is no reliable paper-and-pencil, or biological, predictor of near-term lethality, the clinician has to rely on statistical correlations, hand-me-down aphorisms, and a gut feeling of potential imminent danger.

The ratio of risk taken to rescuability can be an important clue to the patient's lethality during a very recent attempt. With an instantly lethal attempt (gun), if there is no one present to struggle or haggle with, the patient has the highest risk and the lowest rescuability. Fifty-five percent of all suicides use this method. Jumping from a tall building or bridge can be just as fatal. Other fatal methods involve taking considerably more than an LD_{50} of a tricyclic antidepressant or lithium and using a plastic bag over the head, along with an assumed name in a motel in a distant town. On the other hand, a patient swallowing a fistful of Valium in front of a partner has a far higher rescuability and a much lower lethality.

Another way of understanding the extent of a patient's lethality without asking directly (because a help-repudiator, still intent on killing himself or herself, would be prone to lie) is to ask of a patient that, for example, has overdosed: "Were you surprised at surviving?"

Patients surprised obviously were highly lethal at the time of the attempt. A follow-up question, some minutes later, might be: "Are you disappointed at surviving?"

The presence of other potentiating factors (above) are also of use in making the decision to hospitalize, with or without the patient's consent.

An obvious criterion for mandatory hospitalization is a psychotic patient that has just made a suicide attempt, even if trivial. Other instances include a person over age 40 that has made a first suicide attempt, an individual from a pernicious psychosocial environment that has just made an attempt, and a patient with very strong suicidal ideation with both a plan and the intent.

For the patient hospitalized in medical or surgical service following a suicide attempt, close follow-up with medication and psychotherapy may actually preclude transfer to a psychiatric service. By the time the patient no longer needs to be on the medical or surgical service, if there has been a good therapeutic alliance and good response to psychopharmacological intervention, often the patient can be discharged directly to outpatient care. Sometimes, patients that were drunk when they made a lethal attempt, and without a severe depression before an attempt, do not need transfer to an inpatient psychiatric service. The proviso here is that the patient has been followed closely by the psychiatric consultation service, has been observed to have become euthymic, and is genuinely surprised that he or she made the attempt. Some patients who were drunk at the time of the attempt will buy into the argument that they are now "allergic" to alcohol.

WORKING WITH THE VERY DEPRESSED OUTPATIENT OR ER PATIENT

The often-used contract for safety, often abbreviated in charts as CFS, may give false reassurance for the evaluating clinician. CFS itself has no clinical validity. It should be seen as one part of a comprehensive treatment plan, but it is the clinician's responsibility to evaluate the patient's overall suicide risk and ability to participate in the overall treatment plan.

The major benefit in proposing a contract for safety is to see how the patient reacts to the contract. But beware that the help-repudiator, with a clear lethal drive, can lie through this one without flinching. Moreover, a patient that contracts for safety can be completely undone by a malevolent social environment or alcoholic intoxication.

Finally, let's consider the case of a severely depressed patient that does not have the energy to commit suicide and contracts for safety. By day 10 of a recovery the antidepressant may be working sufficiently that the patient has regained his or her energy, looks better to others, and has increased expectations. At the same time, the patient is still very depressed and feels hopeless. Indeed, hopelessness and dysthymia may be the last of the depressive symptoms to dissipate. This type of scenario can lead to a marked transient increase in lethality. Alternatively, another pernicious scenario is that the depressed patient may actually not be a unipolar depressive but rather a bipolar depressive, and flips into a dangerous mixed depressed-manic state with perturbation, which can rapidly lead to an increase in lethality.

If one's outpatient calls and seems to be seriously lethal, still refusing hospitalization, it is always best to call 911 and let the authorities and family deal with the dilemma. Most of all, one should act in accord with one's conscience and gut instincts.

Chapter 22

The Depressed Patient That Is or Wants to Become Pregnant

In this quick-grab chapter, we focus on the pharmacological and psychological aspects of working with the patient that has discovered that she is pregnant. The obvious questions are *why, how, what,* and *when.* First, let's do some background on the *why* of pregnancy.

Why is the patient pregnant? Was this a planned and desired pregnancy? Half of all pregnancies are unplanned. In order to understand some aspects of the patient's feelings about being pregnant and whether the patient wishes to carry the pregnancy to term, it is important to understand the context.

Next, let's focus on the *how* of pregnancy. Of the various methods of contraception, birth control pills are nearly 100% effective when consistently used, but 8 in 100 women on the pill still get pregnant in a year's time. The lower-dose hormone formulations may have fewer side effects, but missing a dose by even six hours puts a woman at serious risk of being pregnant; missing two days means there is no effective prevention against pregnancy. Fifteen percent of women who rely on condoms get pregnant each year, usually because of their inconstant use. Coitus interruptus has a 25% chance of pregnancy in a year's time. Of women requesting an abortion, 60% said they used contraception the month that they got pregnant; the other 40% said they used birth control, but not that month, usually because they hadn't expected to have sex when they did.

The *what* of the pregnancy refers to what are the alternatives to carrying the fetus to full term and rearing the child. One in three American women under the age of 45 has an abortion during her lifetime. There are 1.3 million abortions performed each year in this country. Four in 10 pregnancies are terminated by abortion.

Just 7% of abortions occur each year in minors; abortions are mainly an adult problem. Most abortions, 92%, occur in women who said they were using birth control.

Finally, the *when* of pregnancy is important. Is the patient continuing to equivocate or procrastinate about an abortion into the second trimester? Is the woman on a Class D (potentially toxic to a fetus) mood-stabilizing drug like divalproexic (Depakote ER) during the first trimester? Although some women seem to know within days that they are pregnant, surveys indicate that most women do not determine that they are pregnant until they have missed a period, and the fetus is at the sixth week of gestation. At this stage, some fetal exposure to psychoactive medication has already occurred if the patient was taking medications.

Counseling a patient on whether or not to get an abortion, aside from the religious, ethical, and perhaps legal issues, should never reflect the therapist's values. Rather, the clinician's task is to be informative about medical information but neutral about what to do, while helping the patient to develop her own individual creative way of handling this pregnancy at this particular time.

GENERAL ASPECTS OF PSYCHOPHARMACOLOGICAL MANAGEMENT IN PREGNANCY

Planning for a pregnancy must start long before that egg is fertilized. Step 1 is taking prenatal vitamins, with a good dose of folic acid to avoid neural tube defects. Step 2 is to review all medications to see what risks they may pose to the fetus, and during which trimester that might be. Some experts contend that prescribers should record on the medical record of any woman of potential child-bearing age (from ages 9 to 50) the current use of contraception and adherence to use, plus the potential interest in becoming pregnant within the next year or so.

Should the patient currently be on psychoactive medications at the time she became pregnant, or should she possibly need to be on one or more psychopharmacological agents, there is considerable literature, always being updated, on the risks to the fetus associated with medications. Changes in safety ratings of medications can occur frequently, so an updated Medline check is prudent. For example, paroxetine was the experts' favored medication to use for major depression during pregnancy until 2006, when the FDA, after reviewing years of outcome data, determined that it should be moved from Class C (animal studies show some evidence of fetal damage, usually at high doses, but no evidence of human fetal damage) to Class D (evidence of some human fetal risk). Although these risks are usually relatively low, if that risk happens to your patient's baby, that risk turned out to be very high, and very real.

Obviously, the patient, her obstetrician, and her mental health team must weigh the risks, benefits, and alternatives and produce adequate documentation of the patient's informed consent. As will be discussed below, there are risks to being on certain psychoactive medications, but there are also risks to the fetus and the mother of *not* being treated for a serious mental illness.

RISK OF RELAPSE OF DEPRESSION AND ITS IMPACT

When a woman with a history of severe recurrent major depressive disorder on maintenance antidepressants tapers off her medications proximate to her pregnancy, there is a 67% chance of relapse during pregnancy. During pregnancy, both a Beck Depressive Inventory score of 10 or more and the presence of clear mental strain are independent predictors of recurrence of depression. Moreover, there is a fivefold increase in the risk of a relapse for the woman who has tapered off her antidepressants compared to the woman that has continued taking her antidepressants.

Untreated depression during pregnancy is associated with obstetrical complications and infant behavioral abnormalities. Depressed mothers-to-be may not care for themselves properly, including getting regular prenatal checkups. They may not follow their prenatal instructions as carefully. They may not drink enough water and dehydrate. They may resort to cigarette smoking, or use illicit drugs or alcohol, despite knowing that substances can be teratogenic. They may have heightened ambivalence about carrying the pregnancy to term and even seek an abortion for a much previously desired pregnancy. Psychiatric decompensation can be associated with an increased risk of preeclampsia, placental abnormalities plus low birth weight for age, preterm labor, and fetal distress. Additionally, there is the risk of postpartum depression.

IMPACT OF ANTIDEPRESSANTS ON
THE FETUS AND NEWBORN

It seems clear that the risks to the fetus of maternal depression are increased by the discontinuation of antidepressants, as maternal depression can be toxic to the fetus. The evidence of substitution of nonpharmacological interventions, such as cognitive behavioral therapy, to replace medications during pregnancy is not yet reported on, but appears to have promise.

Current evidence indicates that the risk to the fetus from most antidepressants is very small. There are clear risks of teratogenicity to the fetus from certain mood-stabilizing agents, such as Depakote (10% risk) and lithium (also see Chapter 10). The decision about discontinuation of antidepressants should be tempered by prior history of suicidality, violent or aggressive behavior, psychotic symptomatology, major weight loss, or serious inappropriate judgment.

A large number of well-regarded older studies suggest that antenatal use of selective serotonin reuptake inhibitors (SSRIs) is not associated with an increased risk of birth defects (which are about 3.4% in women who are not seriously depressed and on no medication), or else is associated with a minimal overall increase in risk, although there seems to be a small increase in certain cardiac and neural problems. Of course, what is a small increase in statistical risk may be a calamity when that 1:1,000 risk happens to your patient.

More recent studies have raised the possibility that SSRIs in early pregnancy may increase the normal background risk to a small extent. But it is unclear whether some cases of birth defects may have been associated with mothers that did not take their antidepressants as prescribed or who might have taken benzodiazepines (which can be teratogenic at some phases of pregnancy).

A study of paroxetine during the first trimester has resulted in some small increase in abnormalities, especially ventral septal heart defects, leading to the FDA recently reclassifying paroxetine as Class D (demonstrated human fetal risk). There is also a report of persistent pulmonary hypertension in a few infants exposed to SSRIs after the 20th week of gestation. One recent study matched 9,800 neonates with malformations with 5,900 neonates without malformations, and another matched 9,600 other neonates with malformations with 4,000 neonates without malformations. Bottom line: Neither SSRIs as a group nor individual SSRIs are major teratogens.

Certainly patients and physicians wish that there were clearer lines separating risk from nonrisk. Therefore, patients considering pregnancy need to be informed as appropriate, and that needs to be well documented.

Third-trimester exposure to SSRIs and tricyclic antidepressants (TCAs) has been linked to an increase in perinatal symptoms, including jitteriness, poor muscle tone, weak cry, respiratory distress, hypoglycemia, and in a few cases, seizures. These perinatal symptoms are generally not long lasting or severe. Pregnant women and their physicians should not automatically discontinue SSRIs because of these recent data. There is some evidence that maternal SSRI use is associated with somewhat shortened length of gestation. This risk, however, is not likely to be clinically significant except for women with other risk factors for preterm births (birth before 37 weeks' gestation).

Finally, SSRIs and TCAs, in a limited number of studies, have not been associated with adverse longer-term neurodevelopmental sequelae in exposed children.

The most recent guidelines, published in the April 2008 issue of *Obstetrics and Gynecology*, note the points seen in Table 22.1 about the pregnant patient with mental illness:

BALANCING THE RISKS

The specific issues for each pregnant woman must be based on her individual situation. Depression during pregnancy is not a benign event. One should bear in mind that there is a fivefold increase in the risk of a depressive relapse in women with recurrent major depressive disorder who discontinue their antidepressants around the time of their pregnancy. Depression during pregnancy can affect participation in prenatal care, nutritional intake, and the likelihood of smoking or substance abuse. By contrast, the risk of an infant's developing pulmonary hypertension is 1 in 1,000 of exposed fetuses.

Put another way, the risks of fetal abnormalities in pregnancy without medication in a nondepressed woman is not negligible— more than 3%. That risk is minimally increased if the woman is treated for depression with monotherapy. The risk may be even greater for the fetus if the woman has *untreated* severe depression. None of these three conditions, however, is without some risk: Fortunately, these risks are statistically quite low.

Table 22.1 Medication Use Guidelines

This patient is best managed with a multidisciplinary team.

A single medication at a higher dose is preferred to multidrug therapy.

Paroxetine (Paxil) should be avoided prior to conception because of congenital cardiac malformations, anencephaly, and omphalocele.

Other serotonin inhibitors are not considered to be major teratogens; limited studies from other antidepressants have failed to demonstrate any significant fetal abnormalities associated with their use.

Prenatal use of benzodiazepines increases the risk of oral cleft by 0.01%, and maternal use before delivery can result transiently in the floppy baby syndrome.

Lithium can increase the risk of cardiac malformations by a factor of 1.2 to 7.7, and the overall risk of congenital malformations by a factor of 1.5 to 3. Fetal echocardiograms should be performed on all women exposed to lithium in the first trimester.

Women using lithium for mild bipolar disorder should consider tapering off the medication before conception, whereas women at moderate risk for relapse may stop lithium until organogenesis is complete; women at high risk for relapse may continue lithium throughout gestation.

Neonatal lithium toxicity in the newborn can produce flaccidity, lethargy, and poor suck reflexes.

Valproate (Depakote) and carbamazepine (Tegretol) should be avoided in pregnancy, if possible, because each is associated with a higher risk of fetal anomalies; lamotrogine appears to be a safer choice.

No significant teratogenic effects have been documented with chlorpromazine (Thorazine), haloperidol (Haldol), and perphenazine (Trilafon) in their extensive use, or with second-generation antipsychotic agents.

During breast feeding, SSRI exposure is lower than during pregnancy, and tricyclic antidepressants (except doxepine) are generally safe; the use of lithium is discouraged, but valproate and carbamazepine are probably safe.

Source: Adapted from *Obstetrics and Gynecology*, April 2008.

Chapter 23

Working With the Divorcing Patient

In this quick-grab chapter, we cover a few of the features that might be helpful to keep in mind when your patient is being divorced or is considering divorcing. The statistics about divorce have no credence or value to those entangled in divorce, but for what it's worth, 60% of all marriages that end in divorce do so in the first decade, and more than 80% do so in the first two decades of marriage. Most married couples do have at least one separation.

The divorce rate has gradually been declining, so that by 2006 it had gone back down to the 1970 level. The divorce rate among college graduates has recently dropped to about 20%, which is about half of what the rate is for non-college graduates. This low divorce rate may be somewhat of an artifact, since fewer couples are marrying and more are co-habitating. Moreover, those marrying are older, better educated, and better off financially. However, couples divorcing after 40 or 45 years of marriage are no longer a very rare phenomenon.

The multiple disruptions and outcome of a divorce may, or may not, be ultimately harmful for the children involved. Certainly how the parents handle their shared parenting responsibilities has an important impact in the short term on the children. Patients may ask the clinician for his or her opinion about whether there should be a divorce. But since the clinician lacks the fortune-teller's crystal ball, it is best not to be drawn into this guessing game.

Almost all patients know someone who has gone through a divorce. Therefore, they have access to advice about a lawyer. The clinician is best advised to avoid recommending the names of divorce lawyers.

Some people with depression shy away from getting help for fear that it might prejudice their likelihood of getting child custody. Although the legal workings of each state may be different, what is clear is that a judge would not think a parent has good judgment if there is an evident depression and the parent is not getting professional help for it.

ARE PSYCHOTHERAPY NOTES PROTECTED?

There are certain legal landmarks to keep in mind relevant to the confidentiality of a patient's medical records. In 1996, the U.S. Supreme Court established a federal-level psychotherapist-patient privilege, with the comment that effective psychotherapy depends on an atmosphere of trust in which the patient is willing to disclose emotions, memories, and fears to the therapist.

In 2003 the U.S. Department of Health and Human Services issued more comprehensive medical privacy regulations, as part of the Health Insurance Portability and Accountability Act (HIPAA) Privacy and Security Rules. As a result, physicians are now allowed to keep two types of patient records: regular medical records about medications and a separate set of psychotherapy notes, analyzing or documenting the contents of conversations during private counseling sessions. If kept together, there is a chance that a third party, such as a health insurance plan, might have access to all such material, since if they are paying for the sessions, they can demand access to the patient's medical records. In general, process notes of psychotherapy are not discoverable, although as usual, certain exceptions may apply.

In general, patients are allowed to protect the confidentiality of their records, but that is their privilege, and if the patient tells the therapist to disclose the records, that therapist must do so, although the therapist may file a legal motion to challenge that privilege if the therapist thinks it is not in the patient's best interest.

CONFIDENTIALITY OF MENTAL HEALTH RECORDS IN CHILD CUSTODY CASES

Some patients may fear that their confidential psychotherapy notes might be subpoenaed in a child custody case. One might suppose that psychotherapy notes relevant to a custody issue might enjoy the same type of privileged protection as would be accorded to lawyer-client notes. However, there may be an exception to the confidentiality privilege for mental health records when a parent–child relationship is involved and custody is an issue. (Other exceptions include when a crime has been committed, when the mental health of a party is an issue in litigation, when there is child or elder abuse, and when a suit is filed against a therapist.) Since the laws of each state differ, the patient is best served by getting the question of protection of psychotherapy notes answered by his or her lawyer.

If the clinician does receive a subpoena for psychotherapy records or to appear in person with psychotherapy records in a child custody case, it is important to share that information with the patient immediately so that the patient's lawyer can seek to quash the subpoena. There is usually a defined period of time between the serving of a subpoena and the necessity of handing over records to the court. This allows time to file a motion to quash (to request that the judge disallow the discovery of psychotherapy notes to be used as evidence in the case). Obviously, the best way for the clinician to stay out of trouble is to get legal advice as soon as such legal issues arise.

ECONOMIC IMPACT OF DIVORCE

What is certain is that the costs to support two households after a divorce often go up by 40%. And since income generation in most families cannot expand that rapidly, what happens is that there is less money to go around for both parents and for the children. Often mothers and their children become *nouveau pauvre* (newly poor), with a decline in their standard of living.

COUPLES THERAPY

Couples therapy by an independent clinician, not either of the spouses' mental health caregivers, can often be helpful when the goal is to have either a creative marriage or a creative divorce. In such an instance, the couples therapist takes on the sick marriage as a client. If given an opportunity by both husband and wife, over time and regardless of the marital outcome, couples therapy can be supportive to both parties and can aid in the necessary healing that needs to take place.

Clinical depression, weight gain, increase in drinking, and reversion to smoking cigarettes are all common outcomes of a divorce, no matter whether the patient is the "do-er" or the "do-ee."

When Your Patient (or You) Is Stalked

In this quick-grab chapter we focus on the information the clinician needs to know, quite rapidly, about stalking. Here we define stalking as repeated, persistent, and unwelcome attempts to approach or communicate with the victim. Unwanted telephone calls, letters, gifts, or surveillance make the victim feel exposed, threatened, and powerless. Stalking is meant to violate the boundaries of personal space, and it succeeds.

Even if the stalker does not make overt threats, the stalking instills fear in the victim.

These events come up often, without any warning, in the context, for example, of an acrimonious breakup of a relationship, and the patient will ask for advice on how bad it might get and what to do. Many victims feel the need to alter aspects of their daily lives, including routines, even workplace or living place. They may become anxious, increasing their cigarette smoking or alcohol consumption.

It continues to surprise me how many of my patients are stalked, at least for a few weeks in the midst of a breakup of a significant relationship, or as they are starting a new relationship after a stormy termination. Patients are very upset by constant drive-by surveillance, ceaseless pleading or threatening calls, or flooding of e-mails at home or at work.

Stalking is not rare. Statistics on the matter vary. Community-based studies of stalking victimization report ranges of 12 to 32% for women and 4 to 17% for men. Clinicians are more likely to be stalked than the general public, usually by their patients.

Yet we mental health workers know little about stalking, and rarely, if ever, do academic grand rounds or annual meetings of professional societies devote sessions to this troublesome matter. Therefore, what follows is some bare-bones information on types

Table 24.1 Five Types of Stalkers

1.	Rejected type who pursues an intimate partner, desiring reconciliation or revenge, with a possible criminal assault history and most likely a personality disorder
2.	Resentful type who feels persecuted and desires retribution, intending to frighten or distress the other, due to a specific grievance with paranoid diagnosis
3.	Intimacy-seeking type who desires a relationship with a "true love"
4.	Incompetent type who acknowledges the victim's disinterest but hopes that his or her behavior will lead to intimacy; typically this type of person has a low IQ, is socially inept and has a sense of entitlement.
5.	Predatory type, preparing for a sexual attack, stalks to study and observe; a history of paraphilias and prior sexual offenses is common, and there is no warning before an attack.

of stalkers, how much worry should be associated with some of these types, and what are the options available for intervention.

TYPES OF STALKERS

Conventional wisdom is that there are five types of stalkers (Table 24.1). In a typical private practice, with a depressed woman separating from an abusive relationship, the rejected type of stalker seems to be far more common than the other types. This chapter focuses mostly on the patient dealing with a rejected type of stalker. For other types, the reader can find out more information on the Internet.

FACTORS THAT INCREASE RISK TO PREVIOUSLY INTIMATE PARTNERS

Among other factors, stalking is particularly likely to happen after a breakup, and especially if the victim is starting a new relationship (Table 24.2). The victim is at greatest risk in the midst of legal proceedings that give the stalker intense feelings of humiliation or narcissistic injury. It is best for the stalking victim to be particularly vigilant during the times listed in Table 24.3.

Factors that increase the risk of violence include a prior history of violence, a criminal record (especially for violent crimes), and

Table 24.2 Factors That Increase Risk of Stalking

Substance use

Narcissism

Entitlement

A personality disorder with anger or behavioral
  instability depression with suicidal ideas

Table 24.3 Times To Be Extra Vigilant for the Stalker

The initiation of the restraining order

An arrest of the stalker

Court hearings

Custody hearings

Anniversary dates

Family-oriented holidays

previous threats, especially specific or if made face-to-face. Risk factors for homicide or serious physical harm include previous (unwanted) visits to the victim's home, previous violence during stalking, threats to harm the victim's children, and notes placed on the victim's car.

WHAT CAN THE STALKING VICTIM DO TO PROTECT HERSELF?

Stalking victims of the rejected type can be coached to take responsibility for their safety by becoming familiar with local stalking laws, resources, and law enforcement policies. There are a number of safety strategies, and the person being stalked needs to be assertive in implementing them.

When stalking or abuse begins, the stalker should be given one clear "stay away" message that reflects no ambivalence. It is important that the victim does not carry on any type of subsequent dialogue. Should the stalking then continue, the victim should contact the police and continue to stay in contact with them as the stalking persists.

Collecting evidence is necessary: Keep a diary of subsequent unwanted contacts, save and date the tapes from the answering machine, photograph any physical damage to property, plus keep all letters and e-mails. The victim may wish to establish a post office box for mail, only letting trusted individuals have any information about address, telephone numbers, and e-mail address, and warning them about the stalking. Shred all personal correspondence rather than putting it in the trash. Keep duplicate copies of this material in a safe place if possible.

The victim may need to vary daily routines, even develop optional places to stay if need be, and make plans in case of an emergency if stalking or threatening behaviors escalate.

A restraining order often needs to be obtained. However, each state has different statutes governing stalking; many statutes are being appropriately updated to further protect the victim. For some states, evidence of stalking or cyberstalking is sufficient, but other states require testimony concerning physical harm, sexual harm, or imminent threat for the court to grant a restraining order. The police should know of criteria necessary for a restraining order.

Although most of those that are victimized by multiple daily harassing telephone calls quickly change their telephone to an unlisted number, a clever stalker can usually find the new number within 48 hours. Some experts suggest that the victim should keep the old number as the "stalker's number," buttressed with an answering machine, and either get an additional unlisted land line or use a cell phone for personal use, while recording the harassing calls to use as evidence for prosecution. Major Internet service providers (ISPs) have an address to which subscribers can send complaints of abusive or harassing e-mail. That address usually is "abuse@ISP domain name."

There are also victim advocacy groups, such as Survivors of Stalking, that can give information about services and locations of local safe houses or domestic violence shelters. In some cases, it may even be best to go out of town for a while if that is an option.

Experts warn that the stalking victim, if the stalking continues unabated, should not develop any false sense of security. Rejected stalkers with a lot of investment in the relationship may not be deterred by threat of criminal sanctions. In rare instances, a protective order may escalate stalking and violence, but most research indicates that restraining orders do protect abused women.

WHEN THE CLINICIAN IS BEING STALKED

I have never been stalked and have always listed my home telephone number in the white pages directory. Perhaps I am lucky.

I have known of only one psychiatrist who was being stalked. He told me that he was being seriously harassed by ceaseless telephone calls from a former patient. I may know others who have been stalked, but if so, they never told me. But being stalked is a potential occupational hazard for mental health clinicians. However, the community-based incidence and prevalence of stalking of clinicians is still unknown.

One report found that 5% of a counseling center staff had been stalked by patients they have treated, but 64% had experienced some sort of harassing behavior. Perpetrators in one study were characterized as having personality disorders or paranoid, psychotic disorders. They were further characterized as never having been married, with a history of misuse of drugs and alcohol, and assaultive, fear-inducing, and self-harming behavior. They often have had multiple psychiatric admissions.

Psychiatrists, and those working in related subspecialties, such as forensic psychiatry, may be at higher risk than the general population. One survey of psychiatrists attending a state psychiatric society meeting, using a fairly strict definition of stalking, indicated that a third had been subjected to stalking. Psychologists also are at higher risk than the general public: 10% and 20% of psychologists in two surveys experienced serious stalking events during their careers. Apparently stalking violence to clinicians from their patients is relatively rare. Confronting patients about their behavior, which must be done, may not be particularly helpful.

Although some stalkers of clinicians are disgruntled former patients, some others may harbor unrealistic expectations of intimacy arising from the normal therapeutic relationship: for example, with the intimacy seekers and the incompetent suitors. Erotomania apparently is rather rare.

TREATMENT FOR THOSE STALKING CLINICIANS

This subject is little discussed in the literature. Obviously, the stalking patient needs to be told to stop, and treatment terminated then and there; or else, if given another chance, terminated if stalking persists. Giving the patient names of others to consult for further therapy, to avoid abandonment, poses a serious moral dilemma for the terminating clinician.

Resentful stalkers usually have considerable self-righteousness and are difficult to engage in treatment. Legal sanctions may inflame rather than inhibit their behavior. But apparently many can be persuaded to stop by fines or threats of incarceration. Incompetent stalkers tend to abandon their stalking rather easily, but may start stalking someone else. Intimacy-seeking stalkers must have assertive psychiatric management, particularly because they are impervious to judicial sanctions: They view court appearances or imprisonment as the price they must pay for true love. Finally, predatory stalkers are a problem for the criminal justice system.

Chapter 25

When Tragedy Befalls You or Your Patient

In this quick-grab chapter, we discuss what happens when the unexpected and drastic happens to you. For example, one of your parents dies. Or one of your patients commits suicide. These deaths may be inevitable, usually are not predictable, and are tragic and wrenching. Or you commit malpractice, such as starting lamotrogine (Lamictal) for a patient already on divalproexic (Depakote ER) without using a lowered dosing schedule and the patient develops Stevens-Johnson syndrome.

DEATH IN THE FAMILY

For starters, let's discuss what happens from a professional perspective following a psychiatric resident's hearing of the death of his father. When that happens, whatever protocols he has followed in the past, or even good counsel, may seem far removed.

> The telephone call from a stranger interrupts dinner, informing Dr. Z that his chronically ill and elderly father has taken a turn for the worse and died suddenly—both an expected and dreaded event. The conscientious trainee simultaneously text messages three fellow residents to inform them that his pager has been left at the hospital switchboard, and that he will be leaving the city immediately for an indefinite time span.
>
> Ten days later, while still dealing with distraught family members and issues of his father's estate, the resident remembers that one of his outpatients is about to run out of medication, and so the resident calls the clinic to have some other resident refill that patient's prescription.

Table 25.1 Checklist of Coverage Responsibilities When Rapidly Leaving Town

Pager left at switchboard, or elsewhere, with switchboard being given instructions on whom is to cover

Telephone operator to be informed about coverage plans

Clinic notified in some manner to make cancellations of appointments

On-call nighttime and weekend responsibilities need coverage

Other daytime clinical work needing coverage

Voice mail answering message needs to be changed to indicate lack of availability and who will provide coverage

Chief of clinical service and director of training need to be notified

Although trainees know full well what to do about providing coverage when going on vacation, they may well forget what needs to be done when leaving town for a family emergency. Table 25.1 provides a checklist of what items and tasks a resident needs to take care of stat.

Leaving for a funeral involves the same type of arrangements as leaving for a vacation in Costa Rica, just that the trainee's feelings are far different. The pager needs to have continuous coverage (the trainee on call can fill in until a trainee "buddy" can pick up that beeper to carry around for an indeterminate span and deal with whatever specific tasks have been delegated by the departing trainee). Some tasks are not so readily delegated, like changing one's voice mail message to reflect who is covering for urgent clinical situations and medication refills. The departing resident or the covering resident will need to cancel clinics and cover all on-call responsibilities until further notice. The director of residency training needs to be notified, either directly or indirectly. The e-mail "out of office" message needs to be turned on if at all possible to reflect lack of availability.

Except for the physical transfer of pager from one resident to another (perhaps by way of an intermediary institutional resource), most of the above functions can be performed in less than half an hour, and often can be handled from the airport, between planes or in the car on the way home. In most institutions the voice mail notification can even be handled within a few hours by the resident from a distant point if need be. But "cutting and running" is not an available option, no matter how right it may feel.

The topic of how to cope professionally while dealing with a family disaster may not have been covered explicitly in training sessions. But there still are expectations of what is proper behavior for a clinician. When away from the program for whatever reason, one is expected to just be away from the program, because part-time availability, unless properly prepared for with patients and staff, can be hazardous for patient care.

DEATH OF YOUR PATIENT

Suicide is such a common cause of death in the mentally ill that it is exceptional for a clinician not to have had at least one patient in active treatment that has ended his or her own life. The data are rather daunting: One of 6 deaths of a cohort of bipolar patients is accounted for by suicide; for the addictive disorders, also 1 of 6; for schizophrenia, 1 of 10; and for neurological disorders with a depression or psychotic component, 1 in 10.

Chronic and persistent mental illness and acute, devastating psychiatric disorders can be potentially lethal. True, cardiologists and oncologists are far more accustomed to losing their patients than psychiatrists and psychotherapists. When your patient commits suicide, since so many patients have been struggling with suicidal ideation, with or without plans, with or without intent, it will come as a shock, often with a sense of loss and sometimes even a sense of failure, to hear such bad news.

> Mrs. Q calls, irate, to tell you that your patient, Mr. Q, won't be keeping Tuesday's appointment because he just jumped off the Jamestown bridge. They are still searching for his body, but his fall was witnessed, and his car was left, engine idling, in the breakdown lane.
>
> You tell her how sorry you are. You wonder whether the wife's hopelessness or critical demeanor sparked his leap. You get hold of the chart the next day to write "Case closed" so the chart won't have to come up on the 90-day review of nonterminated but inactive charts. You call back Mrs. Q the next day, after informing the chain of command in your program and hospital, including your supervisor. You ask her if she wants to come to your office at a time convenient for her just to talk (free of charge) after the funeral.

Below is a checklist for residents upon hearing the bad news:

Call the chief resident for suggestions on what protocols need to be followed.

Call the service chief, training director, and supervisor of the
case (whose name will be listed as the clinician of record).
Do not delay in calling the institution's risk management office.
Consider post-vention with the family, free of charge.

Uncommon events still need to be handled administratively in
a common manner. The boss should never end up being surprised
when something untoward happens. Your supervisor and probably
others will need to be debriefed. And aside from the legal aspects of
the case, you will need to talk to others, peers, and experienced men-
tors about what transpired, what you might have missed, what you
might have done differently had there been another opportunity.

The risk management officer will let you know if you need to write
anything more on the patient's chart (never backdate anything)
and whether you will need to be careful about any *mea culpa*
statements. Patient's families do not often sue, but such actions can
be terribly debilitating to all concerned and quite protracted. The
risk management officer, a lawyer, can tell you what is and is not
privileged communication, lest some of your colleagues be inadver-
tently called on for a deposition or even court testimony.

Some psychiatrists have gone to their patient's funerals or memorial services, with the family's prior approval. Letters of condolence
would certainly seem appropriate. Seeing the patient's family in
your office one or several times (without charge or note taking in
their presence) can also often be helpful in developing closure for
the family as well as for the therapist. If prevention didn't succeed,
and if acute intervention was not possible, perhaps post-vention
can help to begin the healing process.

MALPRACTICE

It is estimated that medication errors result in 7,000 deaths in
America each year.

Newspapers tend to pick up on "wrong leg" cases, wrongful
anesthetic deaths, "bad baby" cases, and deaths in young people
sent home from the ER twice before streptococcal pneumonia is
diagnosed and the patient dies the next day. But grieving families
do sue. The literature on malpractice tells us that there is a lot

of botched medical care and untoward outcomes, but those that are sued usually have done a poor job of communicating realistic expectations to their patients and their families.

> Mrs. R has been a compliant and multitalented bipolar II patient that has been stable for the past year on Depakote, which a previous resident had started her on before you inherited the case. Her valproic acid blood levels had been in the therapeutic range, when a six-month slide into depression had jeopardized her significant other relationship, her job, and her health insurance.
>
> A trial on several antidepressants had been futile. She had not been able to tolerate side effects from lithium and had refused atypical anti-psychotic medication, because of both weight gain and her fear of tardive dyskinesia. You elected to add lamotrogine and had had good clinical results recently with four other patients. You told your patient about the rare but very real possibility of an untoward effect, a very severe skin rash.
>
> You told her the likelihood, so you felt she was an informed consumer, and you had documented that you had discussed the risks, benefits, and alternatives of her treatment.
>
> Unfortunately, you neglected to prescribe the half a standard dose of Lamictal (since she was also on Depakote), and two weeks later the patient missed her next appointment because she had been admitted to a general hospital with a severe allergic skin rash, Stevens-Johnson syndrome.

Here's a checklist of what you need to do within the week of such an incident:

Talk to your supervisor about what next to do.

Inform the risk management office of all the particulars of the case.

Inform your chain of command of the adverse outcome and your role in it.

Read over your recent chart notes, but do not backdate any.

See if you were as good at documenting the R/B/A as you were at warning the patient.

Keep in touch with the patient or her hospitalist physician during the medical hospitalization.

When adverse events happen, those patients that have a positive attitude toward their clinician rarely even think of bringing suit.

You had mentioned to the patient, Mrs. R, that you cannot keep her entirely risk-free, and that the consequences of nontreatment seemed quite grave, so accepting treatment was a calculated risk. You work out with your supervisor how to deal with your own role in the patient's allergic response. Along with your fellow residents, you decide to present the case at the quarterly Morbidity and Mortality meeting, for the edification of other residents. This is a Quality Review meeting that is a privileged communication not subject to subpoena.

The patient recovered completely from the hospitalization within 10 days and continued her psychiatric treatment. Her depression lifted while she was in the ICU.

Chapter 26

The Clinician's Vulnerability to Violence

In this quick-grab chapter, we consider what a clinician needs to know about patients' potential for violence toward the mental health clinicians that are treating them. In Chapter 13, this primer dealt with violent patients from a therapeutic perspective: how they should best be treated. In this chapter we deal with issues of clinician safety. Chapter 24 presented the issues of stalking.

Following the tragic bludgeoning death on a Sunday afternoon in 2006 of Wayne Fenton, MD, the associate director of Clinical Affairs at NIMH and deputy editor of *Schizophrenia Bulletin*, by one of his new private patients, clinicians have been forced to revisit the issue of their own vulnerability. Which patients are most likely to turn unexpectedly on their treaters? How vulnerable are we? What can we do to mitigate bad outcomes?

STAFF WORK WITH PATIENTS WITH A HISTORY OF ANGER OR ASSAULTIVE BEHAVIOR

My personal experience with manic patients needing restraints, as well as with patients convicted of assault, is that after the tumult has passed (and there is no longer any stress; the psychosis, if present, has lysed; and the emotions are no longer dysregulated), these patients are as sensitive and empathic as nonviolent patients.

The key to working with patients that show their anger or have a history of anger is to make certain that one is doing things *with* the patient and not *to* the patient. It is imperative to avoid being provocative in any way, and to avoid any perception of a confrontation.

Dr. S was an enterprising, aggressive third-year psychiatric resident in the ER. He drove his well-tended Porsche with assertion: quite fast but responsibly. He could not understand why he was assaulted several times during his ER rotation while none of his more cautious (or timid) fellow residents ever came close to any such encounters.

Personal style is important when dealing with potentially violent patients, and predicting which patients may become violent is no easy matter. Being ever vigilant with undermedicated patients early in an episode is another way for the mental health worker to avoid becoming a victim.

Patients with delusions, sometimes quite hidden, as in schizophrenia, may lash out quite unexpectedly. It may be exceedingly difficult to predict what statement or behavior of the clinician might unintentionally "press their buttons."

Here are some of the facts about violence. Violence is far more likely to happen to our patients than be caused by them. But people with mental illness do commit 5% of the homicides in the United States each year. The *Psychiatric Times* of January 2007 notes that the rate of being a victim of a nonfatal, job-related violent crime is 12.6 per 1,000. Among physicians in general, the rate is 16.2 per 1,000, and for mental health professionals, the rate is 68.2 per 1,000. Moreover, 41% of psychiatric residents in several institutions in Pennsylvania reported that they had been assaulted.

One needs to be extra vigilant when a patient has a past history of assaulting others.

Mr. T was a 24-year-old single Hispanic unemployed male referred to a community mental health center for evaluation after his family brought him to an emergency room. He had stopped his medications and was grossly disabled. He was sleeping poorly and was only rarely eating. He was talking to himself and isolating. He was not deemed a significant threat in the ER and was not sent to an inpatient service, but was referred to a community mental health center (CMHC) as a new outpatient after he was initially calmed by 10 mg of olanzapine. The referral note to the CMHC did include the phrase "He had been violent to other persons in the past."

After he was evaluated by the CMCH psychiatrist without incident, he remained quiet but responsive and made fair eye contact. He tried to give a coherent history but gave few details. He was clearly disturbed enough to merit inpatient care, with a history and mental status examination consistent with the diagnosis of chronic undifferentiated schizophrenia. He agreed that he was upset enough to benefit from more intensive care in a hospital setting.

The urgent care clinic nurse then met with him for a while in an office. Then they went outside to the parking lot to await the mutually agreed upon ambulance that would take him to an inpatient unit where a place had been assured. It was a picture of spring tranquility.

As another quarter hour passed with still no ambulance, the staff psychiatrist ambled out to say hello again to the patient and nurse, and see how things were going along, to make sure the nurse was in no distress, nor was the patient. All seemed calm, so after a brief, pleasant encounter, the psychiatrist returned across the parking lot to the clinic building.

Suddenly, without warning, Mr. T felled the psychiatrist with a flying tackle and attempted to strangle him. Fortunately, the nurse was stronger than the patient, and the patient was hauled off the startled psychiatrist.

The patient blurted out that he loved the nurse and was sure that the psychiatrist was trying to steal her from him. At just this point, the ambulance arrived. There were no injuries, except to the elbow of the psychiatrist's seersucker button-down shirt, and the patient calmly got into the ambulance.

When a red flag appeared, as in the case of Mr. T's history of violence toward another person, all staff should have been more alert to the possibility of unexpected violence, no matter how calm the patient may have seemed. The patient had had an initial, calming dose of an antipsychotic agent, but he was still floridly though quietly psychotic. Sometimes our long experience, competence, and centering presence may lull us into thinking that all is just fine. But it may suddenly turn out to be quite the opposite. Both the psychiatrist and the nurse were not cautious enough in the handling of this patient: they trusted their intuition and long experience, rather than making use of a red flag and acting accordingly.

What are the characteristics of assaultive patients? There is no such thing as 100% accuracy in predictions, but probably the best predictor of assault is a prior history of assault. Untreated patients with schizophrenia, especially if they have been using alcohol, can be a problem if they are made anxious or angry by some comment or action that they may relate to in an idiosyncratic manner. Another predictor is that the patient is confused, irritable, boisterous, verbally threatening, physically threatening, or attacking objects.

How can the likelihood of an assault be lessened? If there is any question of out-of-control behavior, you should have one or more mental health professionals or the patient's family members accompany you in the examining room. Place your chair closest to the door and leave the door open if you think you might need to summon help. Do not have any sharp, hard-edged objects that could be seized and used aggressively. Ask to have a panic button installed on the side of your desk. If you discover that the patient has a gun or knife with him or her, do not ask that the weapon be given to you; do not reach for it. Rather, have the patient place the weapon on a table, desk, or the floor, so that you can then retrieve it without any seemingly threatening gesture made toward the patient.

TAKE-HOME POINTS

Look out for history of violence, especially toward mental health staff.

Be cautious with untreated patients with schizophrenia, especially if they have been drinking.

Be alert to the possibility of trouble if the patient is threatening, boisterous, or confused.

Make sure your office is a safe enough place for an interview of a new patient.

Appendix
Useful References

PREFACE

Castelnuovo-Tedesco, P. (1986). *The twenty-minute hour: A guide to brief psychotherapy for the physician.* Arlington, VA: American Psychiatric Press.

Court, J., & Smith, F. (1999). *Making a Killing: HMOs and the threat to your health.* Monroe, ME: Common Courage Press.

Dewan, M. (1999). Are psychiatrists cost-effective? An analysis of integrated versus split treatment. *Am J Psychiatry, 156*, 324–326.

Duffy, F., Zarin, D., et al. (2001). Integrated versus split treatment: Pharmacotherapy and psychotherapy for mood disorder [Abstract]. *Acad Health Services Policy Meeting, 118*, 52.

Green, H. (1964). *I never promised you a rose garden.* New York: Henry Holt & Co.

Goldman, W., & Burns, B. J. (1998). Outpatient utilization patterns of integrated and split psychotherapy and pharmacotherapy for depression. *Psychiatric Services, 49*, 477–482.

Lindner, R. (1955). *The fifty-minute hour: A collection of true psychoanalytic tales.* New York: Rinehart.

Mojtabai, R., & Olfson, M. (2008). National trends in psychotherapy by office-based psychiatrists. *Arch Gen Psychiatry, 65*, 962–970.

Schmidt, C. W. (2004). *CPT handbook for psychiatrists* (3rd ed.). Baltimore: Johns Hopkins Press.

Thase, M. E. (1999). When are psychotherapy and pharmacotherapy combinations the treatment of choice for major depressive disorder? *Psychiatric Quarterly, 70*, 333–346.

CHAPTER 1: BEGINNINGS—NOT A MOMENT TO SPARE

Battaglia, J. (2007). 5 keys to good results with supportive psychotherapy: Evidence-based technique gains new respect as a valuable clinical tool. *Curr Psychiatry, 6*, 27–34.

Caplan, J. P., & Stern, T. A. (2008). Menomics in a nutshell: 32 aids to psychiatric diagnosis. *Curr Psychiatry, 7*, 27–33.

Gordon, C., & Riess, H. (2005). The formulation as a collaborative conversation. *Harvard Rev Psychiatry, 13*, 112–123.

Madann, V., Kohli, P., & Khuranba, G. (2007). Psychiatric assessment: A word to the WISE. *Curr Psychiatry, 6*, 122.

Nasrallah, H. A. (2006). Medications with psychotherapy: A synergy to heal the brain. *Curr Psychiatry, 5*, 11–12.

Otto, M. W., Smits, J. A. J., & Reese, H. E. (2005). Combined psychotherapy and pharmacotherapy for mood and anxiety disorders in adults: Review and analysis. *Clin Psychol Sci Practice, 12*, 72–86.

Tasman, A., Riba, M. B., & Silk, K. R. (2000). *The doctor-patient relationship in pharmacotherapy: Improving treatment effectiveness.* New York: Guilford Press.

Winston, A., Rosenthal, R. N., & Pinkster, H. (2005). *Introduction to supportive psychotherapy.* Arlington, VA: American Psychiatric Publishing.

CHAPTER 2: MEASURING SYMPTOMS

Rush, A. J., First, M. B., & Blacker, D. (2008). *Handbook of psychiatric measures* (2nd ed.). Arlington, VA: American Psychiatric Publishing.

CHAPTER 3: SETTING THE CONTRACT

Bloom, H., & Rosenbluth, M. (1989). The use of psychiatric contracts in the inpatient treatment of the borderline personality disorder. *Psychiatric Quarterly, 60*, 317–327.

Herron, W. G., & Welt, S. R. (1994). *Money matters: The fee in psychotherapy and psychoanalysis.* New York: Guilford Press.

Lewis, L. M. (2007). No harm contracts: A review of what we know. *Suicide and Life Threatening Behavior, 37*, 50–57.

Newman, S. S. (2006). Set 4 ground at the first office visit. *Current Psychiatry, 6*, 106.

CHAPTER 4: DECISIONS, DECISIONS

Schatzberg, A. F., & Nemeroff, C. B. (2006). *Essentials of clinical psychopharmacology* (2nd ed.). Arlington, VA: American Psychiatric Publishing.

CHAPTER 5: PSYCHOEDUCATION/TEACHING

Bauml, J., Pitschel-Walz, G., et al. (2007). Psychoeducation in schizophrenia: 7 year follow-up concerning rehospitalization and days in hospital in Munich Psychosis Information Project study. *J Clin Psychiatry*, *68*, 854–861.

Burgess, W. (2006). *The bipolar handbook: Real life questions with up-to-date answers*. New York: Avery Publishing.

Colum, F., & Lam, D. (2005). Psychoeducation: Improving outcomes in bipolar disorder. *Eur Psychiatry*, *20*, 359–364.

Miklowitz, D. J., et al. (2003). A randomized study of family-focused psychoeducation and pharmacotherapy in the outpatient management of bipolar disorder. *Arch Gen Psychiatry*, *60*, 904–912.

Pickett-Schenk, S. A., Lippincott, R., et al. (2008). Improving knowledge about mental illness through family-led education: The journey of hope. *Psych Services*, *59*, 49–56.

Toprac, M. G., Rush, A. J., et al. (2006). Implementation of the Texas Algorithm Project and family education program. *J Clin Psychiatry*, *67*, 1362–1372.

CHAPTER 6: SHORTCUTS: HOW TO END ON TIME

Carmody, T. J., Rush, A. J., et al. (2006). Making clinicians' lives easier: Guidance on use of the QIDS self-report in place of the MADRS. *J Affective Disorders*, *95*, 115–118.

Charles, S. C. (2007). Malpractice distress: Help yourself and others survive. *Curr Psychiatry*, *6*, 23–35.

Connor, K. M., Davidson, J., Foa, E., et al. (2000). Psychometric properties of the Social Phobia Inventory (SPIN): New self-rating scale. *Brit J Psychiatry*, *176*, 379–386.

Kung, S., & Lapid, M. I. (2007). Online clinical resources: To pay or not to pay. Free references invaluable in many clinical situations. *Curr Psychiatry*, *6*, 72–81.

Mago, R., Mahajan, R., & McFadden, R. (2007). Help your patients keep appointments. *Curr Psychiatry*, *6*, 77–78.

Mitchell, A. J., & Selmes, T. (2007). A comparative survey of missed initial and follow-up appointments to psychiatric specialties in the United Kingdom. *Psychiatric Services, 58,* 868–871.

Internet resources:

www.searchmedica.com (abstracts and some free entire articles)

www.nlm.nih.gov/medlineplus > Drugs and Supplements (good drug handouts for patients)

http.highwire.standford.edu > Journals (like PubMed, but more free articles in their entirety)

www.medscape.com/psychiatry/journals > Journals and References > Drug Interaction Checker

www.epocrates.com (for office PC or PDA, essentials of meds, doses, interactions)

www.bipolar.org (Gary Sachs, MD, of MGH, very informative site)

www.drugstore.com (sometimes the lowest prices for medications)

www.costco.com (lists their prices, which patients can use for comparison)

www.fingertipformulary.com (a free and user-friendly site to discover if a patient's insurance will cover medication, and if so in which tier, and if preauthorization is needed, by selecting state and insurance company)

www.needymeds.org (For patients that cannot afford their medications, this free site is sponsored by pharmaceutical companies with links to sites for application forms and groups that can help patients fill out necessary paperwork.)

http://medicine.iupui.edu/flockhart/table.htm (Cytochrome P450 interactions; set printer to "landscape" rather than the default "portrait")

www.guggenheim.yourmd.com (my Web site, supported by Medem for the American Psychiatric Association; a basic Web site to assist in psychoeducation for my patients)

www.webmd.com (useful patient information)

Organizations with vetted Web sites:

www.aa.org (Alcoholics Anonymous)

www.adaa.org (Anxiety Disorders Association of America)

www.ndmda.org (National Depressive and Manic Depressive Association)

www.miminc.org (Madison Institute of Medicine; info about lithium, anxiety and affective disorders)

www.niaaaa.nih.gov (alcohol disorders)

www.nami.org (National Alliance for Mental Illness)

www.nida.nih.gov (addictive disorders)

www.nimh.nih.gov (up-to-date research on mental health disorders)

www.ocfoundation.org (Obsessive Compulsive Foundation)

www.psych.org > Psychiatric Practice > Practice Guidelines (for members of the American Psychiatric Association or subscribers of psychiatryonline) www.theniadd.org (National Association for the Dually Diagnosed)

www.trich.org (Trichotillomania Learning Center, Inc.)

Rating scales, easily downloaded (but these Web sites do change often)

Abnormal Involuntary Movement Scale (AIMS): www.atlanta-psychiatry.com/forms/AIMS.pdf

ADHD Self-Report: http://healthnet.umassmedu/mhealth > Tests for Patients

CAGE Questionnaire: www.patient.co.uk/showdoc/40025275

Geriatric Depression Scale: www.stanford.edu/~yesavage/GDS.english.short.score.html

Mood Disorder Questionnaire: www.psycheducation.org/depression/MDQ.html

Patient Health Questionnaire-9: www.depression-primarycare.org/clinicians/toolkits/materials/forms/phq9

Quick Inventory of Depressive Symptomatology (Self-Report), QIDS-SR 16: www.ids-qids.org

Social Phobia Inventory: http://healthnet.umassmed.edu/mhealth > Tests for Patients

Yale-Brown Obsessive Compulsive Scale (Y-BOCS): www.atlanta-psychiatry.com/forms/YBOCS.pdf

Yale-Brown Obsessive Compulsive Symptom Checklist: http://healthnet.umassmed.edu/mhealth/YBOCSymptomChecklist.pdf > Tests for Patients

CHAPTER 7: EARLY AND LATER PITFALLS

Howland, R. H. (2008). Medication adherence. *Psychiatric Ann*, *38*, 323–326.

Lacro, J. P., & Jeste, D. V., et al. (2002). Prevalence of and risk factors for medication non-adherence in patients with schizophrenia. *J Clin Psychiatry*, *63*, 892–909.

Norcross, J. C., & Guy, J. D. (2007). *Leaving it at the office: A guide to psychotherapist self-care*. New York: Guilford Press.

Riba, M. B., Balon, R., & Gabbard, G. O. (2005). *Competency in combining pharmacotherapy and psychotherapy: Integrated and split core competencies in psychotherapy*. Arlington, VA: American Psychiatric Press.

CHAPTER 8: TERMINATING TREATMENT

Cuccuare, M., & O'Donohue, W. T. (2008). *Terminating psychotherapy: A clinician's guide*. New York: Routledge.

Joyce, A. S., et al. (2007). *Termination in psychotherapy: A psychodynamic model of processes and outcomes.* Washington, DC: American Psychological Association.

Roe, D., et al. (2006). Client's reasons for terminating psychotherapy: A quantitative and qualitative inquiry. *Psychol Psychotherapy Theory Res Practice,* 79, 529–538.

Roe, D. (2007). Timing of psychodynamically oriented psychotherapy termination, feelings about therapy and satisfaction in therapy. *Psychol Psychotherapy,* 35, 443–454.

CHAPTER 9: WORKING WITH THE DEPRESSED PATIENT

Aiken, C. B. (2007). Pramipexole in psychiatry: A systematic review of the literature. *J Clin Psychiatry,* 68, 1230–1236.

Beck, A. (2008). The evolution of the cognitive model of depression and its neurobiological correlates. *Am J Psychiatry,* 165, 969–977.

Belmaker, R. H., & Agam, G. (2008). Major depressive disorder. *N Engl J Med,* 358, 55–68.

Bilsker, D., & Peterson, R. *Antidepressant skills workbook* (2008). Downloaded for free at www.comh.ca/antidepressant-skills/adult

Burns, D. D. (1999). *Feeling good.* New York: Harper Collins.

Cooper-Karaz, R., et al. (2007). Combined treatment with sertraline and liothyronine major depression: A randomized, double blind, placebo-controlled trial. *Arch Gen Psychiatry,* 64, 679–688.

Crossley, N. A., & Bauer, M. (2007). Acceleration and augmentation of antidepressants with lithium for depressive disorders: Two meta-analyses of randomized, placebo-controlled trials. *J Clin Psychiatry,* 68, 935–940.

Fava, M. (2007). Augmenting antidepressants with folate: A clinical perspective. *J Clin Psychiatry,* 68 (Suppl. 10), 4–7.

Fawcett, J. (2008). What have we learned from the Systematic Treatment Enhancement Program for Bipolar (STEP-BD) Study? *Psychiatric Ann,* 38, 450–456.

Ghaemi, S. N. (2008). Treatment of rapid-cycling bipolar disorder: Are antidepressants mood stabilizers? *Am J Psychiatry,* 165, 300–302.

Golden, R. N., Nemeroff, C. B., et al. (2005). The efficacy of light therapy in the treatment of mood disorders: A review and meta-analysis of the evidence. *Am J Psychiatry,* 162, 656–66.

Lisanby, S. H. (2007). Electroconvulsive therapy for depression. *N Engl J Med,* 357, 1939–1945.

Marcus R. N., Thase, M. E., et al. (2008). The efficacy and safety of Aripiprazole as adjunctive therapy in major mood disorder: A second multicenter, randomized, double-blind, placebo-controlled study. *J Clin Psychopharmacol, 28*, 156–165.

Miklowitz, D. J. (2008). Adjunctive psychotherapy for bipolar disorder: State of the evidence. *Am J Psychiatry, 165*, 1408–1419.

Nemeroff, C. B. (2008). Fostering foster care outcomes. *Am J Psychiatry, 65*, 623–624.

Oepen, G., Federman, E., & Akins, R. (2006). Measuring outcomes in psychiatric private practice using outpatient self-reports. *Psychiatric Times, 23*, 7.

Parker, G., et al. (2006). Omega-3 fatty acids and mood disorders. *Am J Psychiatry, 163*, 969–978.

Parry, B. (2008). Perimenopausal depression. *Am J Psychiatry, 165*, 23–27.

Pies, R. (2007). How long to wait for an antidepressant to work? *Curr Psychiatry, 7*, 62–65.

Rush, A. J., et al. (2006). Acute and longer-term outcome in depressed outpatients requiring one or several treatment steps: A STAR*D report. *Am J Psychiatry, 163*, 1905–1917.

Rush, A. J. (2007). STAR*D: What have we learned? *Am J Psychiatry, 164*, 201–203.

Sharma, V. et al. (2005). A closer look at treatment resistant depression: Is it due to a bipolar diathesis? *J Affect Disord, 84*, 251–257.

Schwartz, T. L., et al. (2007). How to control weight gain when prescribing antidepressants. *Curr Psychiatry, 6*, 43–54.

Thase, M. E., Rush, A. J., et al. (2007). Cognitive therapy versus medication management in augmentation and switch strategies as second-step treatments: A STAR*D report. *Am J Psychiatry, 64*, 739–752.

Wyche, M. C., Carpenter, L. L., et al. (2007). Neurostimulation therapies for depression: Acute and long-term outcomes. *Depression: Mind and Body, 3*, 106–114.

Zisook, S., et al. (2008). Sequenced Treatment Alternatives to Relieve Depression (STAR*D): Lessons learned. *J Clin Psychiatry, 69*, 1184–1185.

CHAPTER 10: WORKING WITH THE BIPOLAR PATIENT

Basco, M. R., & Rush, A. J. (2007). *The bipolar workbook: Tools for controlling your mood swings* (2nd ed.). New York: Guilford Press.

Farrelly, N., Sachs, G., et al. (2007). Recent advances in the treatment of bipolar depression. *Clin Approaches Bipolar Disorders, 6*, 20–27.

Fawcett, J., et al. (2007). *New hope for people with bipolar disorder: Your friendly, authoritative guide to the latest in traditional and complementary solutions.* New York: Three Rivers Press.

Fieve, R. R. (2006). *Bipolar II.* New York: Rondale Press. Mainly for patients and families, as well as clinicians, a book that focuses on bipolar spectrum disorders.

Forty, L., Smith, D., et al. (2008). Clinical differences between bipolar and unipolar depression. *Brit J Psychiatry, 192,* 388–389.

Frank, E., et al. (2006). The importance of routine for preventing recurrence in bipolar disorder. *Am J Psychiatry, 163,* 981–985.

Frye, M. A., Altshuler, L., Post, R., et al. (2007). A placebo-controlled evaluation of adjunctive Modafinil in the treatment of bipolar depression. *Am J Psychiatry, 164,* 1242–1249.

Ghaemi, S. N. (2008). Treatment of rapid-cycling bipolar disorder; Are antidepressants mood destabilizers? *Am J Psychiatry, 165,* 300–302.

Goodwin, F., & Jamison, K. R. (2008). *Manic-depressive illness* (2nd ed.). New York: Oxford University Press.

Howland, R. H. (2007). Lithium: Underappreciated and underutilized. *Psychiatric Ann, 37,* 619–621.

Jackson, W. C., et al. (2007). Managing bipolar disorder from urgent situations to maintenance therapy. Part 2. Focus on maintenance. *J Clin Psychiatry, 68,* 1290–1300.

Jamison, K. R. (1993). *Touched with fire: Manic depressive illness and the artistic temperament.* New York: Free Press.

Ostracher, M. J. (2008). Subsyndromal depression: Help your bipolar patients feel better. *Curr Psychiatry, 7,* 39–51.

Sachs, G., Nierenberg, A. A., & Calabrese J. R. (2007). Effectiveness of adjunctive antidepressant treatment for bipolar depression. *N Engl J Med, 356,* 1711–1722.

Schneck, C. D., Thase, M. E., Sach, G. S., et al. (2008). The prospective course of rapid-cycling disorder: Findings from the STEP-BD. *Am J Psychiatry, 165,* 370–377.

Suppes, T., Hirschfeld, R. M. A., et al. (2002). Texas Consensus Conference Panel on Medication Treatment of Bipolar Disorder 2000. The Texas implementaion of medication algorithms: Update to algorithms for treatment of bipolar I disorder. *J Clin Psychiatry, 63,* 288–299.

CHAPTER 11: WORKING WITH THE ANXIOUS PATIENT

Kinrys, G., Pollack, M., et al. (2005). Levetiracetam as adjunctive therapy for refractory anxiety disorders. *J Clin Psychiatry, 66,* 870–886, 2005; see also *68* (2007): 1010–1013.

Koran, L. M., et al. (2007). Practice guideline for the treatment of patients with obsessive-compulsive disorder. *Am J Psychiatry, 164,* Suppl.

Leckman, J. F., & Block, M. H. (2008). A developmental and evolutionary perspective on obsessive- compulsive disorder: Whence and whither compulsive hoarding. *Am J Psychiatry*, *165*, 1229–1233.

Mayo Clinic. www.mayoclinic.com/health/caffeine/AN01211

McHugh, R. K., Otto, M. W., & Shear, M. K. (2007). Cost-efficacy of individual and combined treatments for panic disorder. *J Clin Psychiatry*, *68*, 1038–1044.

Pull, C. (2007). Combined pharmacotherapy and cognitive-behavioral therapy for anxiety disorders. *Curr Opin Psychiatry*, *20*, 30–35.

Smith, L. L., & Elliott, C. H. (2002). *Overcoming anxiety for dummies.* Hoboken, NJ: Wiley. (Has been well received by patients as a self-help book.)

CHAPTER 12: WORKING WITH THE TRAUMATIZED PATIENT

Bennett, W. R. M., Roy-Byrne, P., et al. (2007). Can medications prevent PTSD in trauma victims? *Curr Psychiatry*, *6*, 47–55.

Bryant, R. A., et al. (2008). Treatment of acute stress disorder: A randomized controlled trial. *Am J Psychiatry*, *65*, 659–667.

Raskind, M., et al. (2007). A parallel group placebo controlled study of Prazosin for trauma nightmares and sleep disturbance in combat veterans with post- traumatic stress disorder. *Biological Psychiatry*, *61*, 928–934.

CHAPTER 13: WORKING WITH THE ANGRY OR VIOLENT PATIENT

Abderhalden, C., et al. (2006). Predicting inpatient violence using an extended version of the Broset-Violence-Checklist: Instrument development and clinical application. *BMC Psychiatry*, *6*, 17.

Eichelman, B. S., et al. (1995). *Patient violence and the clinician.* Washington, DC: American Psychiatric Press.

Freedman, R., et al. (2007). Psychiatrists, mental illness and violence. *Am J Psychiatry*, *164*, 1315–1317.

CHAPTER 14: WORKING WITH THE SOMATIZING PATIENT

Afari, N., et al. (2005). Chronic fatigue syndrome in practice. *Psychiatric Ann*, *35*, 350–369.

Barsky, A. J., et al. (1998). A prospective 4- to 5-year study of DSM-III-R hypochondriasis. *Arch Gen Psychiatry*, 55, 737–744.

Goldberg, D. L. (2008). Introduction: Fibromyalgia and its related disorder. *J Clin Psychiatry*, 69 (Suppl. 2), 4–34.

Marcangelo, M. J., & Wise, T. (2007). Resistant somatoform symptoms: Try CBT and antidepressants. *Curr Psychiatry*, 6, 101–115.

Neimark, G., Stinnett, J. L., et al. (2005). Medically unexplained physical symptoms. *Psychiatric Ann*, 35, 298–316.

Woolfolk, R., & Allen, L. (2006). *Treating somatization: A cognitive behavioral approach.* New York: Guilford Press.

CHAPTER 15: WORKING WITH THE PATIENT WITH MILD SCHIZOPHRENIA

Davis, J., & Leucht, S. (2008). Has research informed us on the practical treatment of schizophrenia? *Schizophrenia Bull*, 34, 403–405.

Jones, P. B., et al. (2006). Randomized controlled trial of the effect on quality of life of second- vs first-generation antipsychotic drugs in schizophrenia: Cost Utility of the Latest Antipsychotic Drugs in Schizophrenia Study (CUtLASS 1). *Arch Gen Psychiatry*, 63, 1079–1087.

Lieberman, J. A., et al. (2005). Effectiveness of antipsychotic drugs in patients with chronic schizophrenia. *N Engl J Med*, 353, 1209–1223.

Manschreck, T. C., et al. (2008). Schizophrenia recovery: Time for optimism? *Curr Psychiatry*, 7, 40–58.

Nasrallah, H. A. (2008). Is schizophrenia recovery a 'myth'? *Curr Psychiatry*, 7, 19–20.

Newcomer, J., et al. (2007). Severe mental illness and risk of cardiovascular disease. *JAMA*, 298, 1794–1796.

Newcomer, J. (2007). Metabolic considerations in the use of antipsychotic medications: A review of recent evidence. *J Clin Psychiatry*, 68, 20–27.

Swartz, M., Lieberman, J. A., et al. (2008). What CATIE found: Results from the Schizophrenia Trial. *Psychiatric Services*, 39, 500–506.

Wykes, T., et al. (2008). Cognitive behavior therapy for schizophrenia: Effect sizes, clinical models, and methodological rigor. *Schizophrenia Bulletin*, 34, 523–537.

CHAPTER 18: WORKING WITH THE ELDERLY PATIENT

Howe, E. (2007). Initial screening of patients for Alzheimer's disease and minimal cognitive impairment. *Psychiatry*, 4, 24–27.

Spar, J. E., & La Rue, A. (2006). *Clinical manual of geriatric psychiatry.* Arlington, VA: American Psychiatric Press. (This is a wonderful, well-written textbook, with very good references.)

CHAPTER 19: WORKING WITH THE BORDERLINE PERSONALITY PATIENT

Clarkin, J. F., Kernberg, O., et al. (2007). Evaluating three treatments for borderline personality disorder: A multiwave study. *Am J Psychiatry, 164,* 922–928.
Gabbard, G. O. (2007). Do all roads lead to Rome? New findings on borderline personality disorder. *Am J Psychiatry, 164*:853–855.
Gunderson, J. G. (2008). Disturbed relationships as a phenotype for borderline personality disorder. *Am J Psychiatry, 164,* 1637–1639.
Linehan, M., et al. (2006). *Dialectic behavior therapy with suicidal adolescents.* New York: Guilford Press.
Pinto, O. C., & Akiskal, H. S. (1998). Lamotrogine as a promising approach to borderline personality disorder: An open case series without concurrent DSM-IV major mood disorder. *J Affective Disorders, 51,* 333–343.
Siegle, G. J. (2007). Brain mechanisms of borderline personality disorder at the intersection of cognition, emotion and the clinic. *Am J Psychiatry, 164,* 1776–1779.

CHAPTER 20: WORKING WITH THE MILDLY MENTALLY RETARDED PATIENT

Bouras, N. (1999). *Psychiatric and behavioural disorders in the developmental disabilities and mental retardation.* Cambridge, MA: Cambridge University Press.
Harris, J. (2006). *Intellectual disability: Understand its development, causes, classification and treatment.* New York: Oxford University Press.
McCreary, B. (2005). *Developmental disabilities and dual diagnosis: A guide for Canadian psychiatrists.* Kingston, Ontario: Queen's University Press.
Mental Health Aspects of Developmental Disabilities, a quarterly journal, www.mhaspectsofdd.com.
Weber, L., & Wimmer, S. (1986). *Mental illness in persons with mental retardation: ARC facts.* Arlington, TX: Association for Retarded Citizens.

CHAPTER 21: WORKING WITH THE SUICIDAL PATIENT

Hirschfeld, R. M., et al. (2000). Perceptions and impact of bipolar disorder: How far have we come? Results of a National Depressive and Manic Depressive Association 2000 survey of individuals with bipolar disorder. *J Clin Psychiatry, 64*, 161–174.

Jamison, K. R. (2000). Suicide and bipolar disorder. *J Clin Psychiatry, 61*, 47–51.

Kroll, J. (2000). Use of no-suicide contract by psychiatrists in Minnesota. *Am J Psychiatry, 157*, 1684–1686.

Maris, R., et al. (2000). *Comprehensive textbook of suicidology.* New York: Guilford Press.

Reid, W. H. (2005). Law and psychiatry: Contracting for safety redux. *J Psychiatric Practice, 11*, 54–57.

Rudd, M. D., et al. (2006). The case against no-suicide contracts: The commitment to treatment as a practice alternative. *J Clin Psychol, 62*, 243–251.

CHAPTER 22: THE DEPRESSED PATIENT THAT IS OR WANTS TO BECOME PREGNANT

ACOG Practice Bulletin 92: Use of psychiatric medications during pregnancy and post partum. (2008). *Obstetrics Gynecol, 111*, 1001–1020.

Cohen, L. S. (2007). Treatment of bipolar disorder during pregnancy. *J Clin Psychiatry, 68* (Suppl. 9), 4–9.

Freeman, M. P. (2007). Antenatal depression: Navigating the treatment dilemmas. *Am J Psychiatry, 164*, 1162–1165.

Greene, M. (2007). Teratogenicity of SSRIs—Serious concern or much ado about little? *N Engl J Med, 356*, 2732–2733.

Parry, B. (2008). Perimenopausal depression. *Am J Psychiatry, 165*, 23–27.

Payne, J. L. (2007). Antidepressant use in the post-partum period: Practical considerations. *Am J Psychiatry, 164*, 1329–1332.

Stowe, Z. N. (2007). The use of mood stabilizers during breastfeeding. *J Clin Psychiatry, 68* (Suppl. 9), 22–28.

CHAPTER 23: THE DIVORCING PATIENT

Bernet, W., & Ash, D. R. (2007). *Children of divorce: A practical guide for parents, therapists, attorneys, and judges* (2nd ed.). Malabar, FL: M.J.S Krieger.

CHAPTER 24: WHEN YOUR PATIENT
(OR YOU) IS STALKED

Lamberg, L. (2001). Stalking disrupts lives, leaves emotional scars: Perpetrators are often mentally ill. *JAMA, 286,* 519–523.

Knoll, J. (2007). Stalking intervention: Know the 5 stalker types, safety strategies for victims. *Current Psychiatry, 6,* 31–38.

McIvor, R. J. (2006). Stalking of mental health professionals: An under-recognized problem. *Brit J Psychiatry, 188,* 403–404.

Mullen, P. E. (1999). Study of stalkers. *Am J Psychiatry, 156,* 1244–1249.

U.S. Department of Justice Violence Against Women Office. (2001). *Stalking and domestic violence: Report to Congress.* NCJ, 186157.

CHAPTER 26: THE VULNERABLE CLINICIAN

Bataglia, J. (2006). Is this patient dangerous? 5 steps to help clinicians prepare for violent behavior and improve safety. *Curr Psychiatry, 5,* 15–32.

Index